This May Help You Understand
The World

Published in Great Britain in 2007 and the United States in 2008 by
MARION BOYARS PUBLISHERS LTD
24 Lacy Road London SW15 1NL
www.marionboyars.co.uk

Distributed in Australia and New Zealand by
Tower Books Pty Ltd, Unit 2, 17 Rodborough Road, Frenchs Forest,
NSW 2086 Australia.

Printed in 2007
10 9 8 7 6 5 4 3 2 1

The publisher has made every effort to verify that the information
presented in this book is accurate.

A CIP catalogue record for this book is available from the British Library.
A CIP catalog record for this book is available from the Library of Congress.

ISBN 978-0-7145-3137-3
Set in Bembo 11/14pt
Printed in England by Cox and Wyman
Cover design by Holly Macdonald

This May Help You Understand

The World

by Lawrence Potter

MARION BOYARS PUBLISHERS
LONDON ~ NEW YORK

To Joan Potter

CONTENTS

THE ENVIRONMENT: TROUBLE IN THE GREENHOUSE

ISRAEL AND PALESTINE: ROAD MAPS AND WRONG TURNS

DARFUR: AGGRIEVED ACRONYMS

RUSSIA: STORM IN A TEACUP

I AM NOT STUPID

I am not stupid. OK – I admit that I was never going to make it into NASA, and I don't think that it is going to be me that first cracks nuclear fusion. But I can complete most Sudoku puzzles, I once almost won a pub quiz and my school results were decent. So why is it that I feel foolish when I read the newspapers, or watch the news, or find myself in one of these conversations about 'current events' that people have when they have finished talking about the weather?

I know that I am not alone in feeling this way. Many of my friends – some of whom have actually won pub quizzes and are holding down responsible jobs – have also felt humiliated by their own lack of knowledge about world events.

An example. I have a good friend (call her Lola) who is currently writing her PhD on a particular aspect of monkey anatomy. There is no doubt that she has plenty of brain power. I met up with Lola for a drink after work one day, and found that she was unusually quiet. It turned out that she had just come back from a disastrous weekend with her boyfriend's family.

Initially, all went smoothly. Everyone sat down to a hefty dinner, at which there was plenty of conversation, to which Lola contributed fully. She even made her boyfriend's father laugh a couple of times – a notoriously difficult feat to achieve, since most of the time he is only interested in telling his audience about his crucial role in the local Neighbourhood Watch. In case you are interested, he is responsible for preventing the local youth from committing criminal behaviour (such as picnics and ball games) on the well-manicured green at the centre of his village.

Eventually, after a tedious story about hooliganism involving deck-chairs, talk turned towards the parents' holiday plans. They were considering going somewhere exotic. Various locations were suggested – the Bahamas, Peru, East Africa or Thailand. The father mentioned a permanent and inexplicable hankering for Sri Lanka. The problem was, he said, that he was a little worried by reports of the Tamil Tigers.

Now, Lola might specialise in monkeys, but she has a broad interest in all mammal species. She thought that she was familiar with pretty much all of them, and yet here was her boyfriend's father talking about a tiger species of which she had no knowledge. So, quite reasonably, she asked if the Tamil Tiger was indigenous to Sri Lanka, or whether it was also found on the Indian subcontinent.

At a stroke, all of Lola's spadework was undone. You see, the Tamil Tigers are not in fact a big cat species, but a militant group fighting against the Sri Lankan government for an independent state. There was a silence as vast as the Indian Ocean at the dinner table, and Lola felt as if she was falling forwards and downwards into its innermost depths. The father had an expression of incredulity on his face. The mother made soft clucking noises. Even the boyfriend shifted his chair surreptitiously away from his stricken partner. Lola was isolated in her ignorance of current affairs.

But when you examine Lola's crime, it is difficult to see why it should lead to a verdict of ignorance. She was simply lacking a piece of information about a situation which had no direct relevance to her everyday existence. It is as unreasonable to make some sort of judgement about her overall intelligence based on her understanding (or not) of Sri Lankan politics, as it would be to judge a professor of politics by quizzing him on the mating rituals of the various primates.

The thing is we all lead busy lives. We all have jobs to go to. I know that I try to keep on top of what is going on in the world. I glance through the papers most days, and sit down with the Sunday paper at breakfast. I catch the news a couple of times a week. Occasionally, very occasionally, I watch a documentary. Still, despite all these efforts, I don't feel I actually know very much.

There are several reasons for this, I think. Firstly, papers rarely give much background to events. For example, before the Palestinian elections in January 2006, I had a vague awareness of the existence of an organisation called Hamas. After its victory in these elections, Hamas was suddenly front page news. Yet, when I read articles about these important events, I was given, at best, a couple of sentences of background about the organisation. Normally, it was only two or three words: 'Hamas, the militant organisation' or 'The Islamist movement, Hamas'. Knowing that Hamas was militant and Islamist did not help me at all to understand how the movement had won an election.

More fundamental than that, newspapers exist to supply us with facts. Front page stories tell us what has happened somewhere around the world, and not why it has happened. There is little attempt to link an individual event to the wider context. Tragic as it is that a coachful of Sunni Muslims have been blown up by a suicide bomber in Baghdad, a description of this horrific event does not bring us any closer to an understanding of the environment in which it took place. If anything, it drives us further away. We view it from an appalled distance.

I don't know about you, but, for me, the result of all this is an overwhelming sense of helplessness. I know that I don't know enough about what is going on in the world. I feel embarrassed and guilty at my own ignorance. So, I take the only path open to me – withdrawal. I simply refuse to venture an opinion about any worldwide event on the basis that I don't have enough knowledge to do so.

Never is that helplessness felt more keenly, as when you encounter one of those people who have cut-and-dried opinions about international news. I am not talking about journalists or academics or politicians. They are paid to know about this stuff. No – I am talking about somebody who, despite spending their day in a hospital, or an office, or a municipal waste storage site, appears to have found enough time to have sewn up the issues of the day which so perplex the rest of us.

For example, conversation may have drifted seamlessly from the current weather conditions to a discussion of global warming. This is a very common course for conversations to take nowadays in the UK, since any weather pattern can be taken as conclusive proof that the atmosphere is in a state of permanent meltdown. This allows the British to shamelessly indulge both their obsession with the weather and their pessimistic world view at the same time.

Anyway, putting aside analysis of the British psyche, you find yourself involved in a discussion on global warming. It is an uncomfortable enough position as it stands. You are fully aware that you are venturing into territory with which you are not familiar. Your only comfort is that you can see that your partners in conversation feel the same way.

Maddeningly, there is always one person in such a situation who feels none of the nagging doubt that you experience. This person is quite happy to declare point-blank that global warming is the result of increased sunspots, and that human global warming is a conspiracy made up by environmental scientists to keep themselves in well-paid jobs. When challenged, this person will have approximately two facts with which to defend their theory.

The frustrating thing is that a linkage of two facts is easily a powerful enough weapon to defeat anybody else's views on the subject. There is absolutely no chance that anyone else involved in the discussion is going to be able to rustle up a counter-argument. And so this confident person is able to go on their infuriating way with their black-and-white world view unruffled, whilst the rest of us return to the relative safety of an analysis of house prices in our area.

Well, there came a time when I couldn't let this state of affairs continue. Or, more accurately, a period of time arose in my life when I didn't have anything to do. I figured that world events are like any other subject. They just need a bit of study. So, I sat down with the morning paper and wrote down all the questions that floated into my head as I read through it. I asked my friends and relations to do the same. Over time, the list of questions grew and grew and grew. It became clear that I was going to have to focus on just a few areas, and that many of the questions would remain unanswered, not least the true nature of a Tamil Tiger.

Armed with my list of questions, the next step was to go out into the world and find some answers. I felt like a primary school student who has somehow ended up in a university lecture. I was terrified of saying the wrong thing. Despite my fears, I found that academics, journalists, politicians, researchers, diplomats and NGO workers were all very willing to help me out – with a few frosty exceptions (no names). They pointed me in the direction of relevant books, articles and websites. They answered my questions once. They answered my questions twice. They answered my questions a third time. Gradually, issues began to make a bit more sense.

Now, I know what you are thinking. Why should you trust my answers, given that I am a beginner in the arena of world events? Well – I am a thorough kind of person, the kind of person that doesn't like to get things wrong, the kind of person who checks their bank slips against their monthly statement. I can assure you that I made every possible effort to check the facts and opinions that I came across in my research. On top of that, all of the articles have been given the 'all clear' by experts in the relevant areas.

And so here they are – fifty-seven answers to fifty-seven questions that any self-respecting person might ask about the world they inhabit. I hope that, after reading through them, you will have an added confidence when you open the newspaper in the morning, or find yourselves talking about the ongoing security situation in Iraq with a group of strangers at a friend's barbecue. I don't want any of you to end up in the same situation as Lola. We all need just a little more information. I hope that this book is a small step towards providing it.

Lawrence Potter, 2007

IRAQ: BEWILDERED OF BAGHDAD

WHAT IS *JIHAD*?

'The most excellent *jihad* (struggle) is that for the conquest of self.'
Muhammad Hazrat

'*Jihad*' is one of those words that gets bandied about a fair amount
in Western newspapers. Journalists assume that we understand the
concept. More worryingly, we think we understand it ourselves.
Until recently, if you had asked me, I would have confidently
assured you that '*jihad*' was synonymous with 'holy war'. In reality,
its meaning is far more complicated and can describe a variety of
very different actions.

The word '*jihad*' literally means 'to struggle'. Early references
to *jihad* in the Qur'an, and in the hadith (sayings attributed to
Muhammad that were written down much later), do tend to link
it with warfare of some type, either defensive warfare to repel the
threat of an attack against the Muslim community, or aggressive
warfare to extend the dominion of Islam. The early Muslims were
obviously quite good at this kind of thing because, by the end
of the 16th century, they had managed to spread their religion
throughout the Middle East and into Africa, Europe, India and
Southeast Asia.

In modern times, the word *jihad* has taken on a variety of
meanings. It can certainly be applied to a war fought to defend a
Muslim community against an external aggressor. In this situation,
it is the duty of Muslims to defend their faith. However, there
is much more controversy over whether it condones offensive
warfare. The most extreme view is that it is the duty of Muslims

to attack any community that does not operate according to the rules of Islam but calls for a general *jihad* of this type have never been respected by the majority of Muslims. At the beginning of the First World War, the Ottoman Empire called for a *jihad* against the UK, France, Russia and their allies, declaring that it was every Muslim's duty to fight, but this call to war was largely ignored by anyone other than its own subjects.

In general though, the majority of Muslims would say that war is only permissible when there is a clear threat to a Muslim community, either in terms of physical violence or in terms of some kind of hindrance to that community's ability to follow the teachings of their religion. Even then, there are strict rules governing warfare. On the practical side, it is not necessary to fight if the enemy has a force of more than twice your strength – better to regroup and build up your numbers than be massacred. On the moral side, it is not acceptable to kill non-combatants, nor to fight with other Muslims.

If any of these conditions for proper *jihad* are not met, then the warfare is no longer *jihad* and does not meet with the approval of religious authorities. Obviously then, it is important to show that what you are doing meets the requisite conditions, especially since a person who dies during *jihad* can expect all kinds of rewards in the afterlife whereas someone who dies in an unsanctioned war can expect to be punished. The Muslim community as a whole would condemn the action of suicide bombers, because they are not observing the rule that they should avoid the killing of non-combatants. Groups involved in conflicts that result in the death of other Muslims are anxious to establish that those other Muslims have compromised their faith, either by practising an incorrect version of it, or by allying themselves with powers who are demonstrably the enemies of Islam.

However, *jihad* has also come to cover other activities outside the sphere of war. It can be applied to a peaceful 'struggle' to build a better and more just world. Under this interpretation, a teacher who fought against prejudice in the classroom, or a politician who aimed at reducing poverty in society, could both be said to be engaging in *jihad*.

Jihad is also often used to describe a personal struggle against the temptations of the world. A human being is constantly battling against corrupting influences, either internal or external, in order to make the correct moral choices. In fact, many Muslims subscribe to the view that every aspect of life involves *jihad* and that *jihad* is really only the struggle to live one's life according to the teachings of Islam. They would say that of the various ways to engage in *jihad*, *jihad* through warfare is the least important.

Politicians, of course, play on the ambiguities inherent in the word. Yasser Arafat called for a *jihad* to liberate Jerusalem in 1994. By doing so, he was able to satisfy extremist groups who interpreted his words as a threat of physical war, whilst at the same time he could allay the fears of his partners in the peace process, arguing that he was talking about the non-violent struggle to find a solution to the problem.

WHAT IS THE DIFFERENCE BETWEEN SUNNI AND SHIA MUSLIMS?

'Why do you ask me these questions at five o'clock?'
Representative Silvestre Reyes, Chair of the House Intelligence
Committee upon being asked by a journalist whether
Hizbollah was Sunni or Shia

Given the sectarian nature of the current fighting in Iraq, you would think that US policy makers would have some idea about the answer to this question. Worryingly, though, some of them aren't exactly up to speed. During 2006, the *New York Times* reporter Jeff Stein went around asking some of them exactly this question. One of his victims was Terry Everett, a US Congressman and vice chairman of the House Intelligence Subcommittee on Technical and Tactical Intelligence.

Apparently, Mr. Everett responded to the question with a low chuckle. Then, he thought for a moment. Finally, he replied: 'One's in one location, another's in another location. No, to be honest with you, I don't know. I thought it was differences in their religion, different families or something.'

Reid then kindly gave Everett a brief run-down of the basic differences between the two groups. 'Now that you've explained it to me,' Everett replied, 'what occurs to me is that it makes what we're doing over there extremely difficult, not only in Iraq but that whole area.'[1]

What Congressman Everett didn't know is that about 90% of the world's population of Muslims is Sunni, and that Sunnis are the majority Muslim group in the vast majority of Muslim countries. Shias account for most of the remaining 10% of the Muslim population. They are the majority in Iran, Iraq and possibly Yemen, and they form significant minorities in many Middle Eastern countries.

Like Protestants and Catholics, Sunni and Shia are not generally separated along ethnic lines and there are no differences in day -to-day wear. The name might give you something of a clue – for example, many Shias are called 'Ali' in memory of the first imam – but no name is used exclusively by either of the sects.

Still, there are important differences between the two groups, all stemming from the original schism in the Muslim faith caused by the argument over the rightful successor to Muhammad after his death in 632 AD. Some sources say that Muhammad wished the leadership to remain within his bloodline, and that, to this end, he nominated his son-in-law, Ali, as his successor. Other sources say that he died without nominating anyone, and that therefore the successor should be chosen by democratic methods.

The controversy rumbled on for a while, as the leadership of the Muslim faith passed from one person to another, until it ended up in the hands of Ali himself. You would have thought that this would satisfy all concerned, but this was not the case. Ali spent much of his rule fighting against rivals for his position, chief amongst them a man called Mu'awiyah. By the time of Ali's death in 661 AD (the result of losing an argument with a poisoned sword), Mu'awiyah had built up such a following that he was asked to become the next leader, despite the fact that Ali had two sons, Hasan and Husayn, who had legitimate claims to the position.

It all kicked off again after Mu'awiyah died. Most of the Muslim community accepted Mu'awiyah's son, Yazid, as their next leader, but Ali's son, Husayn, refused to recognise his rule. Along with seventy-two followers, he was on his way to the town of Kufah in modern-day Iraq, which had sent him messages of support, when he ran into four thousand soldiers sent by Yazid. Husayn was killed, and his head was sent to Yazid.

And that was where the initial split in Islam arose. The Shias believed that the Muslim leader should belong to the bloodline of Muhammad. They saw Ali and Husayn as his immediate successors, and gave them the title of imam. They were the first in a line of imams, each of which claimed to be the descendant of Muhammad. Arguments concerning the rightful heir led to splits in the Shia movement, and the formation of particular sects. The Shias viewed the imams as mediators between themselves and Allah. The imams were infallible, and worthy of religious devotion.

The Sunnis, on the other hand, were happy for the leadership of the Muslim community to pass to whoever proved themselves most capable of protecting it. They gave their leader the title of caliph. The leadership of the Sunni community quickly became disputed, and various leaders laid claim to it. The Sunnis saw their leaders as fallible human beings. They were worthy of respect, but not religious reverence.

Over the years, despite the distance of the original cause of the split and the fragmentation and eventual demise of the positions of both the imams and the caliphs, the Shias and Sunnis maintained their individual identities. More often than not, the Shias were an impoverished minority, who portrayed themselves as the defenders of the weak against injustice and tyranny. They were often subject to oppression. As a result of this, the Shias developed the practise of 'taqiyya', in which it is perfectly acceptable to conceal your faith in order to avoid persecution. Unsurprisingly, the Shias tended to attract other disaffected groups. In contrast, the Sunnis tended to form the establishment of the various Middle Eastern States.

In modern times, both groups continue to maintain their different identities. Partly as a result of the causes of the original split, and partly as a result of their separate evolutions over history, there are now significant differences between Shias and Sunnis.

Most importantly, Shias look back to the imams and revere them as religious figures. They accord particular devotion to Husayn and Ali, viewing them as martyrs to the Shia cause. As a result, Najaf and Karbala (which are the locations for the tombs of Ali and Husayn respectively) are as important to Shia Muslims as the other Muslim holy cities.

In addition, they attach special importance to the Muslim festival of Ashura, because it was at that time that Husayn was killed. For the Shias, the festival of Ashura is a time of mourning and sorrow. They share in the suffering of Husayn by beating and cutting themselves, and they represent his death through the medium of passion plays.

Sunnis, whilst respecting the role that Ali and his family played in the early years of the Muslim faith, disagree with the special status that the Shias give them. They also disagree with the reverence which Shias continue to show to their religious leaders. For a Sunni, such reverence is misguided as it should be directed solely towards Allah. Sunni religious leaders are there to advise and to give guidance, but Sunnis believe it is possible to communicate with Allah without their help.

Other differences between the two sects arise from a difference between the sources to which they look for religious instruction. The Qur'an is the most important source of guidance for both of them, but it does not contain the answer to all questions. For issues on which the Qur'an makes no ruling, Muslims must consult the hadith, which record the traditions and sayings of Muhammad.

The hadith were initially handed down orally, but they were eventually written down by a variety of people. The two sects have different opinions over which are the most trustworthy sources. For example, the Shia pay particular attention to the hadith of members of the family of Ali, but have no time for the hadith of those who opposed him.

As a result, the two sects have developed some differences in practice. For example, all Muslims pray five times a day, but Shia

Muslims are able to combine some of these prayers into a single session. A busy Shia might get through all the required prayers in three sessions. Shia Muslims allow the practice of fixed-term marriages (called '*mut'ah*'), in which women are paid a fixed sum to become a wife for an agreed period of time, while Sunni Muslims have banned the practice.

However, it is important to stress that the similarities between both groups are much greater than the differences. They both follow the teachings of the Qur'an, they both obey the Five Pillars of Islam, they both revere the same holy cities and they both have the same holy days.

---

1. www.nytimes.com/2006/10/17/opinion/17stein.html?pagewanted=1&ei
=5088&en=c5709ea7c5631b3f&ex=1318737600&partner=rssnyt&emc=rss)

WHY IS THE SUNNI-SHIA SPLIT A PARTICULAR PROBLEM IN IRAQ?

'I say to our Sunni brothers in Iraq that we are brothers and the
occupier divided us in order to weaken the Iraqi people.'
Moqtada Sadr, Shia cleric

Every day, we read about tit-for-tat killings in Iraq between Sunni
and Shia groups. We would be forgiven for thinking that these
two groups have always been enemies, but Sunnis and Shias have
coexisted in Iraq for centuries, and, by and large, they have lived
peacefully together. The Shias form the majority group, but the
Sunnis form a very large minority. Intermarriage between the
two sects was common during Saddam's rule. It is a sad fact that
many of these couples have had to flee the country in fear for
their lives as a result of the mounting sectarian violence.

Historically, the Iraqi regime has been Sunni. Prior to the
country's independence, first the Ottomans and then the British
appointed Sunnis to positions of authority and under Saddam's
rule Sunnis continued to dominate the government. However,
Saddam's regime was not a religious one. He ruled the country
via the mechanism of the Ba'th Party. During his rule, he certainly
oppressed the Shias – for example, he refused to allow them to
celebrate the festival of Ashura – but no more so than he oppressed
other groups that opposed him. In general, both Sunnis and Shias
were happy to see him go.

Given the prior coexistence of Sunnis and Shias, the
development of conflict between the two was unexpected, at

least to the US administration and its allies. Various explanations can be put forward for it. Politically, the Coalition forces have encouraged the Iraqi population to think along sectarian lines. They set out from the start to ensure that the top positions in the government were shared between the Sunnis, Shias and Kurds, rather than allow a totally free democratic process to decide such positions. This might seem like good sense in terms of allowing each group to feel that they have a say, but it meant that the politics of Iraq became defined by religious issues.

In addition, there was no time for the formation of real political parties. The Ba'th Party had dominated Iraqi politics for many years, allowing nothing in the way of viable opposition. With its disbandment by the Coalition forces, there was no political system left. When an Iraqi citizen stepped up to the ballot box, they had no choice but to vote along ethnic lines (in the case of the Kurds) or along sectarian lines (in the case of the Sunnis and Shias). In other words, for the majority of Iraqis, their political choices were decided by their religious background. As a result, rivalry between Sunnis and Shias was built into the political system.

Moreover, the Sunnis had various reasons for feeling that they had not received a fair deal. In a process known as 'debathification', the Coalition forces removed former members of the Ba'th Party from their jobs, and refused them the right to run for political office, work in the military, or hold positions in public services such as medicine and education. Under Saddam, members of the Ba'th Party were mostly Sunnis. However, many Sunnis joined the party simply because it was the only way to be certain of employment and to gain a level of safety in Saddam's regime. They were not part of, or even supportive of, the methods with which Saddam maintained his hold on power. Such people found themselves jobless and excluded as a result of debathification.

There were other problems too. Broadly speaking, Sunnis tend to live in the central section of Iraq and this was the area most disrupted by violence. This meant that voting was a risky affair, or even an impossibility (the US-led attack on Fallujah took place at this time). Other Sunnis did not vote in protest at what they felt to be an unfair election. All of this is in stark contrast to the Shias, who were encouraged to vote by their religious leaders.

As a result, Sunnis feel that they were not fairly represented in the government that drafted the new Iraqi constitution, with which they have serious concerns. In particular, the Sunnis are concerned by the prospect of the decentralisation of Iraq, in which the Shias will control the oil-rich south, the Kurds will control the similarly oil-rich north and the Sunnis will be left with the war-torn central region.

Given all of this, it is not surprising that there are strong sectarian tensions on the political level. However, it still does not explain why there is so much sectarian violence on the street. The problem here is the void left by the demise of the Ba'th Party and with it the Iraqi army and police force. The result has been a collapse of security with various extremist groups taking advantage of this situation to further their own ends. In the absence of a state security system, Iraqi citizens had no choice but to look for protection from their religious leaders, which has resulted in the formation of militias along sectarian lines. It is these militias which are now involved in a cycle of aggression and retribution. The situation is not helped by Iraqi tribal law, in which revenge killing is traditional. Needless to say, the majority of Iraqi citizens do not support the views of these extremist groups, but find themselves caught up in the acts of aggression which they carry out.

Other external forces have become involved. Al-Qaeda has used the situation to further its anti-Western agenda, and there are allegations that Iran is involved, either in an attempt to establish another Shia regime in the Middle East (which will be a useful ally for Shia Iran), or simply to prolong the instability in a country that has traditionally been a rival in the region.

WHAT IS A BA'TIST?

'A day will come when the nationalists will find themselves the
only defenders of Islam. They will have to give a special meaning to
it if they want the Arab nation to have a good reason for survival.'
Michel Aflaq (*In Memory of the Arab Prophet,* 1943)

The papers often referred to Saddam as 'the Ba'tist leader' without
clarifying the nature of this position. I always thought that it
sounded rather sci-fi, imagining Saddam standing in front of rank
after rank of identically dressed 'Ba'ths'. In reality, a Ba'tist is a
member of the Ba'th Party, or to give it its full name, The Arab
Socialist Ba'th Party, which was founded in Syria in 1947 by two
middle-class educators named Michel Aflaq and Salah al Din al
Bitar.

The Ba'tist founders were worried by the influence of Western
powers in the Middle East. They wanted Arab nations to work more
closely together to counter this influence and prevent the decline
of the region as a whole. Their long-term aim was the formation
of a single Arab state, which was to be run along socialist lines.
Hence, the motto of the Ba'th Party: 'Unity, Freedom, Socialism.'

There have been attempts to bring about this ideal. Syria
and Egypt united in 1958 to form the short-lived United Arab
Republic. Syria withdrew from the union in 1961, but Egypt
retained the name until 1971, when it renamed itself the Arab
Republic of Egypt.

The Ba'th Party has branches in many countries in the Middle
East and elsewhere, but it has risen to power only in Syria and

Iraq. It has been the ruling party in Syria since 1963, whilst in Iraq, it came to power briefly in 1963, and then again in 1968, after which it held power until Saddam's fall at the end of the Second Gulf War. However, the branches of the party in the two countries have never been on particularly good terms. Syria supported Iran in its war with Iraq, and was part of the coalition that forced Iraq out of Kuwait in the First Gulf War.

In Iraq, the Ba'th Party came to power by toppling Abd al-Karim Quasim in a coup in 1963. It seems likely that this coup was supported by the US and the UK, who were worried about Quasim's pro-Soviet stance. It is alleged that a shadowy group of the CIA, going by the sinister name of the 'Health Alteration Committee', had already tried to assassinate him by sending him a poisoned monogrammed handkerchief. It is also alleged that the CIA supplied the Ba'tists with lists of names of people who were suspected of communist leanings. The Ba'tists used these lists to help them to round up potential enemies, many of whom were members of the educated middle-class. Around 5000 people were executed during this process. On the day of the Ba'tist takeover, a National Security aide to President Kennedy wrote a note to him saying: 'Almost certainly a gain for our side.'

In the years that followed the coup, the Ba'th Party was subject to in-fighting and temporarily went into decline. However in 1968, after another coup, they returned to power under the leadership of Ahmad Hasan al-Bakr and Saddam Hussein, who set about nationalising the oil industry and introducing social and economic reforms in line with Ba'th Party ideology.

Over time, more and more power fell into the hands of Saddam. Potential rivals were purged from the party, and the party organisation was designed so that all decisions rested with him. Eventually, in 1979, Bakr retired from politics, and Saddam was left in absolute command of the country.

WAS SADDAM'S TRIAL LEGAL?

'The imposition of the death penalty – an inherently cruel and
inhumane punishment – in the wake of an unfair trial
is indefensible.'
Human Rights Watch, November 2006

'Saddam Hussein's trial is a milestone in the Iraqi people's efforts
to replace the rule of a tyrant with the rule of law.'
George Bush at TSTC Airport, Waco, Texas, November 5th 2006

On December 30th, 2006, Saddam Hussein was executed for his part in the Dujail Massacre. On a leaked recording, observers of the execution could be heard taunting the ex-president in the moments before his death. Human rights groups protested both against the use of the death sentence, and the indecent way in which it was carried out. It was the final controversy in a judicial process that had been riddled with problems throughout its duration.

On July 8th, 1982, Saddam visited the small town of Dujail in order to give a speech praising its inhabitants for their assistance in Iraq's conflict with Iran. His convoy was attacked by members of the Shia Da'wah Party and a gun fight ensued, in which Saddam was unharmed.

In revenge for this attack, Saddam's security forces allegedly executed several men on the spot and 143 others after show trials. Some reports say that many more were killed, including women and children. In addition, around 1,500 residents were arrested, the town was demolished and rebuilt, and surrounding farmland was destroyed.

At the time of his execution, Saddam was also standing trial for atrocities committed in the Anfal Campaign against the Kurds in 1988. Further charges were in the process of being prepared on other counts, including the use of chemical weapons against the Kurds at Halabja in 1988, the invasion of Kuwait in 1990, and the suppression of Kurdish and Shia rebellions at the end of the First Gulf War in 1991. All charges against Saddam were dropped after his execution.

There are various opinions on why Saddam was initially tried for a relatively minor incident. The limited scope of the case meant that it was easier to prosecute, and there were witnesses willing to give evidence in court. However, it is also possible that Ibrahim al-Jaafari, the Iraqi prime minister and leader of the Da'wah party at the time, wished to put on a show of strength for his supporters. In addition, some sources suggest that the US was keen to avoid an in-depth analysis of some of the other charges through fear that it might reveal an element of US involvement.

Human Rights Watch, amongst others, registered their concern about the legality of the trial. On the other hand, the vast majority of governments supported it, although many were troubled by the use of the death penalty. According to experts, there were fundamental issues about the legality of the trial from the start.

There is little precedent for the trial of a head of state, but it seems that the structure of the court was a dangerous compromise. Experts say that either Saddam should have been tried in an international court according to international law, or that he should have been tried in an Iraqi court – after an Iraqi system of law had been set up and a judiciary trained. The first option would have given the trial a sense of neutrality; the second would have given the Iraqi people a sense of ownership. As it was, the court was initially set up by the Coalition forces, and then later reaffirmed by the Iraqi government after elections had taken place.

Throughout the process, Saddam was kept in custody at a US base. It was a one-off arrangement that suffered from interference from both the international community and the Iraqi government.

On top of this, once the trial started, it was riddled with problems. Three defence lawyers were assassinated during its course. The chief judge resigned in protest at government interference. Defence lawyers boycotted proceedings on a number of occasions over allegations of unfairness. It is alleged that defence lawyers were not given enough time to prepare a proper appeal. Saddam continually questioned the validity of the court. At his very first appearance, he stated: 'This is all theatre. The real criminal is Bush.' Amidst all this disruption it is difficult to see how it can be said that the defendants were given a fair and unbiased trial.

WHAT DID SADDAM DO TO THE KURDS?

'The tragic struggle of the Kurdish people, which has continued
for so long, originates in the principle of the right of peoples to
self-determination, and for this reason, it is a just struggle.'
Andrei Sacharov, 1989

As it became clearer and clearer that there were no Weapons of
Mass Destruction in Iraq, I remember that there was a period
of time when doubt about the validity of the war was always
silenced by politicians with a stony-faced reference to the plight
of the Kurds. 'Is the war justified?' the politician would ask, and
then say, 'Just go and ask the Kurds.' Some of the audience would
nod and the politician would move on to the next questions,
carefully stepping around the general consensus that we would
have preferred to have been told to talk to the Kurds before we
went to war.

Given the stoniness of the politician's face, I always assumed
that the plight of the Kurds had been pretty bad, but it occurred
to me the other day that I didn't know an awful lot about it. So
I decided to find out exactly what they had suffered at the hands
of Saddam.

The Kurds have been around for a long time. The Greek
historian Xenophon mentions them as 'a fierce and protective
mountain-dwelling people' in his book, the 'Anabasis', written
around 400 BC. Nowadays, there are around 35 million Kurds,
living in an area often referred to as Kurdistan which is made up

of adjoining parts of eastern Turkey, western Iran and northern Iraq. The Kurds are the largest ethnic group in the world not to have their own homeland.

Unsurprisingly, then, they have constantly lobbied to make Kurdistan an independent country. They were promised their own state in the Treaty of Sevres of 1920, but the promise was never fulfilled. The Kurds in Iraq spent most of the last century at war with, or in negotiations with, the powers-that-were in their quest for self-rule. At first, they fought with the British (who ruled Iraq after the First World War), then with the various regimes that ruled the country after its independence, and finally with the Ba'th Party, when it came to power in 1968.

Temporarily, things looked up for the Iraqi Kurds in 1970, when the Ba'th Party leadership promised to give them more autonomy, but this promise too went unfulfilled. A large factor in the regime's refusal to give the Kurds more power was the presence of massive oil fields in Kurdish territory. From this time onwards, the Ba'th Party increased hostilities. They deported thousands of Kurds to other parts of the country, and replaced them with Arabs from the South in an attempt to gain more control of the oil fields. Any resistance on the part of the Kurds was met with violence.

Saddam Hussein took open control of the country after 1979, and, under his leadership, aggression towards the Kurds escalated, culminating in the Anfal campaign of 1988, during which, according to Human Rights Watch, around 2,000 villages were destroyed, hundreds of thousands of Kurds were deported, and tens of thousands more either disappeared or were executed. Human Rights Watch concluded that the Anfal campaign aimed to wipe out the Iraqi Kurds and constituted genocide under the 1948 Geneva Convention.

The most notorious of the atrocities committed during 1988 was the chemical bombardment of the town of Halabjah on March 16th and March 17th. There has been some dispute over who was responsible for the attack, with some authorities pointing the finger at Iran, but most sources now agree that it was Iraqi forces that carried it out.

At the time, the town was under the control of Kurdish and Iranian fighters. (In 1988 Iran was at war with Iraq, and it suited them to support the Kurds in their fight for independence.) Many of the 70,000 inhabitants were in hiding in basements and cellars, as the Iraqi forces bombed the town with conventional artillery. However, this only made them more vulnerable to the chemical bombs that followed, which released gases that tended to collect in low-lying areas. Between 4,000 and 5,000 people died as a result of the effects of mustard gas and nerve agents. Human Rights Watch conducted interviews with survivors who spoke of watching as people 'just dropped dead' or 'died of laughing'. These survivors watched others 'burning and blistering' or 'coughing up green vomit'.

The Anfal campaigns went on after the Halabjah gas attack, and continued to be characterised by cruelty and brutality. Despite this, the Kurds rebelled once more at the end of the First Gulf War (1990–1991), and were again crushed by Iraqi forces. However, this time the international community, who had condemned earlier campaigns without taking any action, stepped in to create a 'safe haven', which, for the most part, the Iraqi government allowed to be self-governing.

WHAT IS THE CURRENT SITUATION WITH THE KURDS?

'The Kurds have a saying; The world is a rose; smell it and pass it
to your friends.'
Justice William O'Douglas, 1950

Given that the suffering of the Kurds under Saddam's regime
was often given as a major reason for the invasion of Iraq, it is
surprising that you don't hear much about them in the papers
nowadays. Northern Iraq – where the Kurds live – is barely
mentioned. It is as if, in all the troubles, the Kurds have been
forgotten. I wondered whether life has been better for them since
Saddam's defeat, or whether they too have been caught up in the
chaos and violence.

In the aftermath of the First Gulf War, the Kurds attempted to
rise up against Saddam once more. Saddam suppressed the uprising
brutally. In order to protect the Kurds from further aggression, the
United States and its allies established a 'safe haven' in Northern
Iraq. From this time on, Saddam largely left the Kurds to govern
themselves. They set up their own regional government, in which
the two dominant parties were the Kurdish Democratic Party
(KDP) and the Patriotic Union of Kurdistan (PUK).

Kurdish forces (known as '*peshmerga*') allied themselves with
the Coalition forces in the Second Gulf War, and continue to
play a security role, having a reputation as impressive fighters. The
Kurdish parties are well-represented in the Iraqi government, and
Jalal Talibani, leader of the PUK, is its new president.

However, the Kurds continue to have their own regional government, with its own president (the KDP leader Massoud Barzani). As a result of the period of relative calm since 1991, the Kurdish region is relatively prosperous, with its per capita income roughly 25% higher than the rest of the country. It has been far less affected by the recent war than other parts of Iraq, and so oil money has been spent on development rather than repairing damaged infrastructure and importing food. The region is also less troubled by sectarian violence. The regional government is even promoting Iraqi Kurdistan as a tourist destination.

The current situation is a strange one. The Kurdish region is not meant to function in such an independent manner – it is meant to be part of the Iraqi state. At the moment, nobody is prepared to challenge the status quo, especially whilst the future of Iraq is so uncertain, but eventually the issue will have to be resolved.

The KDP and the PUK continue to maintain that they wish Iraqi Kurdistan to remain part of Iraq as a whole. However, there is growing discontent with these parties on the Kurdish street. Young Kurds have never experienced anything other than independence, and they now take this for granted. They feel that the two parties are missing the chance to create a legitimate independent state. They are also angered by allegations of corruption in the ruling parties.

There are considerable problems associated with the formation of an independent Kurdistan. Neighbouring countries are very uneasy about it, because of the danger that their own Kurdish populations will push more strongly for independence. In particular, Turkey is unlikely to allow the formation of a Kurdish state, and there is a real danger that it would invade Iraqi Kurdistan to prevent such an entity from existing.

Politicians argue that it is better to remain as part of Iraq, but to push for a federal state, in which Iraqi Kurdistan would remain largely autonomous. However, the current instability in

Baghdad throws doubt on the possibility of any form of stable Iraqi government.

Even now, the Kurdish region is not without its troubles. In particular, there are arguments about the status of the town of Kirkuk, which lies at the edge of Iraqi Kurdistan in an area with large oil reserves. The Kurds would like the town to be the capital of their region, but Kirkuk contains a diverse mix of ethnicities and so there is strong opposition to this proposal.

The situation is made even more problematic by the fact that, throughout his rule, Saddam forcibly removed Kurds from the city, relocating them elsewhere, and replaced them with Arabs from the south of the country in order to strengthen his control over the area. Currently, Kurdish families are returning to their homes whilst Arabs who settled in the city after 1980 are being asked to leave. Unsurprisingly, there is considerable resentment among both groups.

Once this process has taken place – it is scheduled to be finished by December 2007 – there will be a referendum on whether Kirkuk should become part of Iraqi Kurdistan or not.

WHO ARE THE MARSH ARABS AND WHAT ARE THEY DOING NOW?

'We broke the dams when the Iraqi army left. We want to teach our children how to fish, how to move on the water again.'
Qasim Shalgan Lafta, a Marsh Arab and former fisherman who helped restore the water to the Iraqi wetlands that Saddam had destroyed – *Chicago Tribune*, 13th July 2003

I am sure that somewhere at the Labour party headquarters there is a 'List of Reasons to Give to Journalists for Why We Must Go To War with Iraq.' At number one – and probably now crossed out – is Weapons of Mass Destruction. Everyone has heard plenty about them and their non-existence. At number two is the plight of the Kurds. Occasionally we hear about them. And at number three – only ever used to deal with the most persistent of interviewers – is the Marsh Arabs. We never hear about them. Who are they? What have they got to do with marshes? And are they happier now that Saddam has gone?

The Marsh Arabs have been living in the huge marshes at the confluence of the Euphrates and the Tigris in southeastern Iraq for 5,000 years. They may be the descendants of the ancient Sumerians, who may have been the first inventors of the plough and written language. They are mostly Shia Muslims.

As a result of the inaccessibility of the marshes, the Marsh Arab lifestyle changed little over the centuries. Each family constructed an island on which they built their house. They travelled around the marshes in canoes. Children could expect to receive their first boat at six. Septuagenarians paddled around the waterways without anyone asking them if they could read the number plate on the canoe in front.

They kept buffalo for their milk and their dung, but never for meat. Occasionally an animal could be sold to outsiders, but the Marsh Arabs never killed one of their own beasts. It is surprising how many uses there are for buffalo dung. It can be mixed with reeds to make fuel for cooking and heating fires. The smoke from these fires has an acrid smell which helps to ward off insects. It can also be used on roofs to make them waterproof and as a poultice on wounds. However, the Marsh Arab lifestyle was destroyed in the aftermath of the First Gulf War.

Various Shia groups in southern Iraq were encouraged by Saddam's defeat at the hands of international forces, and rose up against him. It seems likely that they were encouraged to do so by US forces, but that the US stopped short at openly assisting them. The rebels were no match for Saddam's forces, and the uprising was quickly and brutally suppressed.

There is little evidence to show that the Marsh Arabs took an active part in the rebellion, but the Marshes provided a hideaway for opponents of Saddam's regime (as they had done for centuries for dissidents and outlaws). To protect his authority, Saddam ordered them to be drained. In the space of a few years, large areas of the Marshes were reduced to 15% of their original size (according to the NGO organisation AMAR). Drained areas quickly turned into inhospitable desert, and the displaced inhabitants were forced to look for a home elsewhere. It is estimated that around 100,000 Marsh Arabs made their way into Iran as refugees.

With the fall of Saddam, there have been attempts to reflood the marshes. In some areas, the ecosystem is recovering but in others it may be permanently damaged due to toxic soil conditions. Even if it is possible for the Marshes to return to something like their former state, it is not clear whether they will be allowed to flourish, given that there are large oil reserves and land for farming in the area, which the government may feel are more important for the country's redevelopment. On top of that, many Marsh Arabs do not want to return to their old homeland, preferring to try and find more profitable lives elsewhere.

FURTHER READING

Allawi, Ali A, *The Occupation of Iraq: Winning the War, Losing the Peace*, New Haven, Yale University Press (2007).

Darwish, Adel and Alexander, Graham, *Unholy Babylon: The Secret History of Saddam's War,* New York St Martin's Press (1991).

Fuller, Graham E. and Franke, Rend, *The Arab Shi'a: The Forgotten Muslims*, New York, St. Martin's Press (1999).

Tripp, Charles, *History of Iraq*, London, Cambridge University Press (2002).

Watts, Montgomery, *What is Islam?*, London, Stacey International (2002).

http://www.islamonline.net/english/index.shtml

http://www.memri.org

http://www.globalpolicy.org

THE USA: SWINGING STATES AND HANGING CHADS

HOW DO THE USA PRESIDENTIAL ELECTIONS WORK?

'You win some, you lose some. And then there's that
little-known third category.'
Al Gore, Democratic National Convention, 2004

'Let's make sure this time every vote is counted.'
Al Gore, 27th July 2004

Everyone over the age of ten or so will remember the controversial
US presidential elections in 2000 and the outrage that greeted
the results. I especially remember news presenters talking about
something called the 'electoral college'. From the gravity with
which they spoke about this entity, it was clear that it played a
large part in the election process. I wondered whether it might be
a special course that hopeful presidents had to attend in order to
study the basic principles of presidential behaviour, rather similar
to the way businessmen attend business schools.

It turns out that there is no such school. On election day, which
is always on the first Tuesday after the first Monday of November,
US citizens vote for their preferred candidate. In 2000, the two
main candidates were Al Gore for the Democratic Party and
George W Bush for the Republican Party, but there were several
others competing on behalf of smaller parties, most notably Ralph
Nader for the Green Party.

Actually, the US citizen is not voting directly for his preferred
candidate. He or she is voting for a group of people who have

47

promised to vote for their preferred candidate on behalf of the citizen's state. These people are called presidential electors. At the end of election day, when each state has chosen its particular group of presidential electors, the chosen presidential electors are referred to as the electoral college.

It is the electoral college that eventually decides who is going to be the president (and who is going to be the vice-president). They always cast their votes forty-one days after election day, returning to the capitals of their respective states to do so. In theory, it is possible for them to go back on their promise, and vote for a different candidate, or to abstain from voting, but in practice this almost never happens which is why everyone knows who is going to be president once the votes have been counted after election day. In 2000, once all the arguments over the 'hanging chads' in Florida had been settled, George W Bush was declared president-elect, even though the electoral college had not yet cast its votes. Just to remind you, 'hanging chads' are pieces of paper left in a poorly-punched hole on a ballot paper, although, in my imagination, I like to think that a gentleman might use the term in a good-natured way to refer to his testicles.

In fact, in 2000, when it came to the voting of the electoral college, one of the presidential electors did refuse to vote. Such an elector is called a 'faithless elector'. Barbara Lett-Simmons, who was representing the District of Columbia, refused to vote on behalf of Al Gore, as she had promised, in protest at the fact that the District of Columbia does not have proper representation in the US Congress. The District of Columbia basically consists of the city of Washington DC, and has only a non-voting representative in the House of Representatives, and no representation in the Senate at all. As a result, license plates in Washington DC carry the legend: 'Taxation Without Representation.' It does seem a bit unfair.

Anyway, whatever the feelings of discontent in the District of Columbia, that is what the electoral college is, and the mechanics of it have a big influence on how presidential candidates conduct their campaign. Different states have a different number of electors. Each state has the same number of electors as it has representatives in the House of Representatives and the Senate combined. So, for example, Idaho, which has two senators and two members of congress, has four electors (or electoral votes) allocated to it, whereas California, which has two senators and fifty-three members of congress, gets fifty-five electors (or electoral votes) in the electoral college. The District of Columbia, to save further trouble, is allocated three electoral votes. Nationally, this adds up to 538 electors in the electoral college.

The situation is further complicated by the fact that the vast majority of states have a first-past-the-post voting system for presidential candidates. In other words, if 49% of the people in California vote for the Democrat candidate, 43% vote for the Republican candidate, and the remaining 8% vote for another candidate (or don't vote at all), then the Democrat candidate will get ALL fifty-five of the votes in the electoral college – even though the Republican candidate received 43% of the popular vote in the state. The states of Maine and Nebraska have different systems, but, as a result of the political make-up of these states, their electoral votes have never been split between the Republicans and Democrats. Due to the way the electoral college system works, it is highly unlikely that a candidate from any of the lesser parties will ever receive any electoral votes, because they would have to receive the most votes in a state to do so. In 2000, Ralph Nader received around 3% of the national vote, but was nowhere near topping the polls in any individual state. However, minor candidates are still able to influence elections. Many Democrats were angry with Nader for running, because they felt that he took away crucial votes from Gore. In some states, the Republicans financed pro-Nader adverts in order to split the Democrat vote.

Another controversial result of the electoral college system is that it is possible for a candidate to receive the most votes nationwide and still lose the election. In 2000, Gore received 500,000 more votes than Bush, but five less electoral votes. This is the third time in US history that such a scenario has taken place, although the other two occasions were in 1876 and 1888.

Finally, the electoral college system means that presidential candidates have a tendency to focus their campaigns on states where the outcome of the popular vote is in doubt. Such states are called 'swing states'. There is no point in a candidate spending resources in persuading more people to vote for them in states that they know they have already won (or lost). For example, a Republican candidate can expect to win Texas and to lose Vermont, and so there is little merit in campaigning heavily in these states.

In 2000, eleven states were decided by less than 4% of the votes cast. These were the swing states. Amongst them were New Mexico, Oregon and Florida, all of which were so close that it was impossible to declare a result for them immediately. At that point, Gore had received 255 electoral votes and Bush had received 246 electoral votes, which meant that the twenty-five electoral votes allocated to Florida would decide the contest. New Mexico and Oregon had too few electoral votes to change the outcome – they were eventually both won by Gore.

So the electoral college is directly responsible for the feverish attention focused on the state of Florida in the 2000 election. When the Supreme Court ruled on December 12th that there were to be no further vote recounts there, Bush was declared to have won the popular vote in the state by just over 500 votes (or less than a hundredth of a percent). He therefore received all 25 of Florida's electoral votes, enough to give him a majority in the electoral college and the presidency.

WHAT IS THE DIFFERENCE BETWEEN A SENATOR AND A CONGRESSMAN?

'The Constitution is not an instrument for the government to
restrain the people, it is an instrument for the people to restrain the
government – lest it come to dominate our lives and interests.'
Patrick Henry (1736-1799), American Revolutionary

Sometimes, I feel a hankering for the simplicity of monarchies.
You knew where you were in the days of William the Conqueror.
If he said 'invade England' you invaded England. If he said, compile
a database of all the landowners in the country, you jumped to it.
The chain of command was simple.

Nowadays, it is all so much more complicated. I know that the
Magna Carta and the French Revolution and the Declaration
of Independence had everyone's best interests at heart, but they
make it harder to know who is making the decisions. Democratic
governments are complicated systems, designed to prevent too
much power resting in any one place. But that means you can't
point at one person any more, and say, 'He told me to do it.'

I have a fairly good idea of how my own government works,
but the workings of the governments elsewhere around the globe
are a mystery to me. On reading the papers, you would be forgiven
for thinking that George W Bush was single-handedly responsible
for every decision that the US government has made since 2001,
but presumably his decisions have come as a result of some kind
of consultative process. For example, if he were to decree that
rodeo should become a compulsory part of the US educational

curriculum, I hope that the American political system might have something to say about it.

Now, I knew that there were such things as senators, and congressmen (and of course, congresswomen), and I suspected that it was part of their job description to keep the president in check, but I did not know how they went about it, or what the difference between them was. I reckoned the difference between a congressman and a congresswoman was probably connected to biology, but I was not so sure that this was the key for explaining the difference between a senator and a member of congress.

It all started with the American Revolution. In 1774, there was a First Continental Congress, in which representatives from various British colonies sent a letter of complaint to King George III. He did nothing about their problems, and so the colonies went to war, set up the Second Continental Congress, and sent him another letter – this time declaring that they would rather be independent of his rule. The letter referred to the various ex-provinces as the 'united States of America', although this was not yet a formal name, which is why 'united' does not have a capital letter. 'States' was only capitalised because, at this point, all nouns in the English language started with capital letters.

Anyway, capital letter or no, the united States of America set up their own government, in which each state sent an equal number of representatives, and each state could veto any decision. This arrangement turned out to be pretty ineffective when it came to making decisions, and so in 1787 a meeting was called in order to work out a new constitution.

There was plenty of argument about what form the new government should take. Unsurprisingly, small states wanted to continue with a system in which every state had equal representation, whereas large states were keen on a system in which each state sent a number of representatives in proportion to its population. It was hard work coming to agreement, but eventually everyone did. It was called 'the Great Compromise'.

Under the Great Compromise, the United States Congress was set up to be the part of the government which passed laws. It contained two houses of equal power. The first of these was the House of Representatives, which contained members of congress, who were elected for two-year terms. The number of members of congress sent by each state was proportional to its population. Every state had at least one representative. The second house was the Senate, which contained two senators from each state, who were each elected to serve six-year terms.

The idea was that the House of Representatives would represent popular opinion, whereas the Senate would be a less impulsive body of proven citizens. As Edmund Randolph, one of the delegates at the convention on the constitution said, the Senate was designed '...to restrain, if possible, the fury of democracy.'

The function of the US Congress remains largely unchanged today. Both the Senate and the House of Representatives examine and debate each potential law (or bill) that is put before it. In order for a bill to pass through Congress, both houses must pass exactly the same wording of it. Once this has happened, the bill is sent to the president, who has all sorts of options. He can sign it and make it law. He can veto it, in which case it does not become law, unless two-thirds of each house vote to overturn the veto. Or he can refuse to sign it, in which case it becomes law after ten days – unless Congress has gone on holiday, in which case it never becomes law. Or he can issue a 'signing statement', which informs Congress that he intends to disregard the law or portions of it. George W Bush has made more use of this option than any other president.

Congress also has other powers. Any international treaty signed by the president must be approved by the senate. The same is true of his choices for various important positions, such as cabinet ministers, ambassadors and judges of the Supreme Court. Recently, the senate has, on average, blocked a couple of appointments by the president each year. The House of Representatives has the power to impeach government officials it suspects of misconduct. The senate passes judgement on such cases. Bill Clinton was the second president to be impeached.

It is still felt that the House of Representatives remains closer to popular opinion, as, in general, the constituency of each member of congress is smaller than that of a senator (although this is not the case in the smallest states), and the term for each member of congress is much shorter. Also, members of congress have less of a tendency to vote against party lines.

Despite these differences, both houses form a check to the power of the president. No law can be passed unless they agree to it – which is why it is unlikely that we will be seeing America's teenagers riding broncos in gym class any time soon.

WHY IS THE NEW HAMPSHIRE PRIMARY SO IMPORTANT?

'New Hampshire is like a suit of long underwear frozen stiff on the clothes line.'
Senator Eugene McCarthy

The New Hampshire primary is part of the process by which the different US political parties choose who is going to be their candidate for a presidential election. Currently, there are several contenders for the Democrat nomination for the 2008 election, amongst whom are Hilary Clinton and Barack Obama. Similarly, the Republican Party has its various contenders, amongst whom are the former New York mayor, Rudy Giuliani and Senator John McCain. The smaller parties also have their candidates.

Over a period of several months, each party will hold a selection process in each state to choose between the various contenders. The nature of these selection processes varies from state to state. Broadly speaking, there are two categories: caucuses and primaries. In a primary, state citizens vote for their favoured candidates, whereas in a caucus state citizens come together in local meetings to nominate representatives who will attend further meetings at county, district and state levels. It is at these later meetings that the various representatives vote for their preferred candidates.

In New Hampshire, each party holds a primary election. The Democratic primary is open to members of the Democrat Party, and the Republican primary is open to members of the Republican

Party. In addition, and unusually, state citizens who are not members of any party are also allowed to vote in a primary, but they are only allowed to vote in one of them. In other words, they can't turn up to the Republican primary and vote for Giuliani, and then wander in to the Democrat primary and vote for Obama.

Once all the votes have been counted, each candidate receives a number of delegates proportional to their share of the vote. So, if Rudy Giuliani receives 60% of the vote in the New Hampshire Republican primary, he will be allocated 60% of the New Hampshire delegates to the Republican National Convention. These delegates are pledged to vote for him at the convention, which takes place after all the states have gone through their selection procedures. It is at the convention that the delegates take the final vote to decide who will be the Republican candidate for the presidency. However, due to all this pledging, the result of this vote is generally known well before the convention has started.

In the same way, if Hilary Clinton receives 30% of the vote in the New Hampshire Democrat primary, 30% of the New Hampshire delegates at the Democrat National Convention will be pledged to vote for her.

There are a couple of further issues. Firstly, there are also New Hampshire delegates from the Democratic Party, who have nothing to do with the primary elections. They are called super-delegates, and gain their place at the convention because they have important roles in the New Hampshire Democratic Party. They are free to vote for whomever they choose. Secondly, many candidates drop out of the race before their party convention. Their delegates are then free to vote for another candidate. Thirdly, a candidate is only allocated delegates if they receive more than 10% of the vote in the primary. If they do not, they get no delegates at all. The total vote of all candidates who fail to reach the 10% mark is given to the winner of the primary election. Nobody ever said it was simple.

The reason why the New Hampshire primary is so important

is because it is the first primary to take place. It provides the first chance for people to judge the performance of the various candidates' campaigns. As a result, it gets huge amounts of media attention and can make or break a candidate's chances. Candidates that perform poorly often have to drop out, whilst candidates that perform well can receive a huge boost to their campaign in the form of higher profile and financial donations. Since the current system was introduced in 1952, the eventual president has only failed to win their New Hampshire primary on two occasions.

In his 1992 campaign for the Democrat nomination, Bill Clinton, although he did not win the New Hampshire primary, came a surprisingly strong second. The result relaunched his campaign, which had been badly damaged by a series of sex scandals in the previous year, and he went on to win the Democrat nomination. In 1996, Steve Forbes spent three million dollars on his campaign in New Hampshire, only to come fourth in the primary. Supporters of the New Hampshire primary say that the state is a good test of candidates. Due to its small size and low population, candidates are able to campaign without access to massive funds, and the population are able to form a detailed view of the different candidates. However, other states are jealous of New Hampshire's position, saying that it does not make sense for it to have such a major influence on the outcome of the contests.

New Hampshire has already had to move its primaries forwards several times over the years to protect their status. Originally, they took place in March. In 2008, they are scheduled to take place on January 22nd. Various states have threatened to move their primaries in front of New Hampshire. In order to protect itself, New Hampshire has suggested that it will insist that all candidates who wish to take part in its primaries must pledge to support its position as the holder of the first primaries. It reminds me of children squabbling to be first in the queue. Why don't they give the honour of staging the first primary to a different state each election? It would be much fairer.

WHAT IS A NEOCON?

'American power should be used not just in the defense of
American interests but for the promotion of American principles.'
William Kristol

Newspaper articles have a habit of slipping the word 'neocon'
into their argument, without necessarily explaining their reasons:
'Bush's neocon strategy', 'Rumsfeld's neocon vision', 'a neocon
belief in military power'. It is one of those words that paints
everything connected to it in a darker light.

A 'neocon' sounds as if it should be a futuristic monster
attacking our planet in a flurry of laser rays. We humans wouldn't
stand a chance against its advanced armour, artificial intelligence
and menacing voice box. The only way I have found to banish this
mental image is to recast a 'neocon' in the form of a cutting-edge
state-of-the-art air-conditioning system – a much less troubling
concept.

Still, there were times when the air-conditioning strategy didn't
do the trick. Eventually I decided that part of the problem was
that 'the neocons' were able to draw on my fear of the unknown.
The newspaper articles never explained what they actually were.
Although many of them hinted that they were indeed hostile
life-forms from another galaxy. It turns out that there is nothing
new about the neocons or 'neoconservatives' to give them their
full name. The first neocons were Democrats or socialists who
became unhappy with both the domestic and foreign policy of
their leadership. At home, they were concerned about the erosion

of moral standards amongst the American people, and abroad, they opposed the policy of negotiating with the communists. Eventually, they changed their allegiance, and supported the Republican President, Ronald Reagan, who took a much more aggressive attitude towards the USSR.

Modern neoconservatives continue to believe in the importance of traditional moral values, and they continue to believe in the importance of confronting external threats aggressively. There is nothing particularly unique about this outlook. Plenty of other people have similar values. Where the modern neocons become controversial is in the way that they currently see the world order, and in the methods that they propose for dealing with it. Modern neocons talk about 'World War Four'. The enemy is no longer communism but Muslim regimes in the Middle East. The ex-CIA director, James Woolsey, at an address to college students at UCLA, stated that the religious rulers of Iran, the 'fascists' of Iraq and Syria, and extremist groups like Al-Qaeda were all enemies of the USA.

In response to this threat neocons are quick to suggest the use of force. They argue that since the end of the Cold War the US remains the only superpower on the world stage and is in a position to influence the world order in a much more direct way than previously. They are perfectly happy to use pre-emptive force against a possible threat, even if this threat is nothing more than a challenge to the US-led world order. Critics suggest that the neocons were well aware that Iraq had no real potential to threaten the US militarily, but that they were simply angered by its opposition to the US. The neocons are also perfectly happy to act without the consent of international organisations, such as the UN.

Various motivations are put forward for the neocon strategy. In recent years, neocons have taken to painting the picture in very idealistic terms, stating that they are simply trying to help other nations move towards the ideals of democracy and the free market, and that they are not afraid to use US military power to achieve this goal. But in general, non-neocon commentators take the view that neocons are simply unafraid to use the US's current military advantage to extend its influence, and they see the Middle East, with its oil, as being the most strategically useful place to do this. A much more controversial view is that many neocons have links with Israel.

Critics of the neocons say that their view of the world is dangerously black-and-white and that it is not possible to operate in such simplistic terms when dealing with foreign relations. For example, labelling Iran as an enemy takes no account of its complicated internal politics, in which many citizens hold pro-Western views. They argue that a 'friend-enemy' world-view blocks the possibility of compromise between countries, and leads to far more confrontation than is necessary.

In addition, they say that it is all very well to talk of spreading democracy, but that it is naïve to think that this is simply a matter of defeating a non-democratic government in a military fight. For example, in Iraq the US had very little difficulty in winning the initial war, but has found it increasingly difficult to help the country rebuild itself. It has certainly not managed to set up a free-market democracy. Apparently, at one point, neocon politicians even considered the suggestion that Islam should not be the religion of the new Iraqi state. Critics say that events in Iraq have show that it is impossible to bring about radical changes in a state in just a few years, and that the US lacks the will to remain involved over the much longer period of time that might achieve such a change.

IS BUSH ACTUALLY STUPID?

'He's dumb like a fox.'
George W Bush's mum

Judging by comments posted on the internet, there are plenty of people out there who are happy to write off Bush's decisions as president as the result of his stupidity. A popular US bumper sticker reads: 'Somewhere in Texas, a village is missing its idiot.' Everyone is able to quote bizarre statements from his speeches. My favourite is: 'I know the human being and fish can coexist peacefully.' And everyone knows the story about how, in his campaign for election in 2000, Bush was unable to name the leaders of important foreign countries, such as Pakistan and India.

But, despite all this, I find that I don't want to accept this as an explanation of the school playground. This is partly because it reminds me too much of the classroom, where any argument, no matter what its causes, can quickly turn into an exchange of slurs on mental capacity and partly because I have a sneaking admiration for a man who is able to take extended holidays despite having the most demanding job in the world.

My admiration for him has only grown – although, I admit, not to levels that excuse his presidential mistakes – since discovering that, in 1966, he was arrested for drunk and disorderly conduct involving the theft of a Christmas tree. I bet Al Gore never stole a Christmas tree. He would have been more likely to deliver a lengthy sermon chastising Christmas tree owners worldwide for encouraging the destruction of the pine wood habitat, and therefore accelerating global warming.

Whatever the moral issues involved in Christmas tree burglary, it seems that the allegations of Bush's stupidity are unfair. In the US, all prospective college students take the SAT reasoning tests, which judge their verbal and mathematical skills. Bush scored 1206 out of 1600. Due to changes in the SAT tests, Bush's score would now be equivalent to around 1280. This puts him in the top 10% of prospective college students. According to several sources, this SAT score suggests that Bush's IQ is around 120, which is the same as that of John F Kennedy.

Bush ended up going to Yale to study history. He happily admits he was a 'C' student there, concentrating more on rugby and his membership of the secretive society The Order of Skull and Bones. Overall, Bush scored an average of 77% for the course he took at Yale. He was particularly good at anthropology, history and philosophy, scoring 88% overall. His grasp of astronomy was not so strong. He notched up only 69%.

During the contest for both the 2000 and 2004 presidency, it was always claimed that Bush's opponent was far cleverer than him. Al Gore did score significantly better in his SATs, with 1355, but scored similar grades to Bush at Harvard. It is hard to find a SAT score for John Kerry (although one figure sometimes given is 1190), but his average at Yale was 76%.

It seems that overall, Bush measures up fairly well in the intelligence department against his two rivals for the presidency. Besides, as several commentators point out, academic intelligence is not the only quality necessary for a president. It might be better to spend time analysing other aspects of Bush's personality.

The problem with this, though, is that there are no objective criteria to make such a judgement. I have found reports which praise him for his 'laser-like ability to reduce an issue to its core.' I have found reports that worry about his reliance on instinct, and his tendency to categorise issues in simplistic black–and–white terms. It is difficult to form a coherent view. All you can say is that, if a man has been elected to the most hotly contested job on the planet twice in a row, he must have some strengths somewhere.

DID THE BUSH ADMINISTRATION LIE ABOUT WEAPONS OF MASS DESTRUCTION?

'The open question is how many stocks they had, if any, and if
they had any, where did they go? And if they didn't have any,
then why wasn't that known beforehand?'
Colin Powell, January 24th 2004

I am not alone in my confusion about why the US and the UK
went to war with Iraq. For months and months, I have listened to
friends trying to come up with an explanation for how the two
governments could invade a country for reasons that turned out
to be totally unfounded. In the build-up to the invasion, the Bush
administration repeated over and over again that it was certain
that Saddam had weapons of mass destruction, and that he was
prepared to use them. In October 2002, Bush said: 'America must
not ignore the threat gathering against us. Facing clear evidence
of peril, we cannot wait for the final proof – the smoking gun
that could come in the form of a mushroom cloud.'

So it came as a big surprise when the invading armies were
not able to find any signs of any of the kinds of weapons that
Bush had been talking about. There were no biological weapons,
no chemical weapons, and no sign of a nuclear programme. As
one member of a task force assigned to finding and destroying
Saddam's WMD said: 'We came to bear country, we came loaded
for bear, and we found out the bear wasn't here.' I think it is safe
to guess that the man was using 'bears' as a metaphor for 'WMD'.

Either that, or there were some serious misunderstandings at the initial briefing meetings for the mission. Assuming that the former explanation is the correct one, how could there be such a massive gap between what the US government has told its citizens and the actual truth?

The most extreme view was that the whole WMD story had been a total invention, that the Bush administration had wanted to go to war against Iraq for other reasons (maybe to extend their influence in the Middle East, maybe for oil), and that WMD were simply an excuse fabricated in order to get the public on board.

The flaw with this argument is that the Bush administration was not the first to state that Saddam was a threat. Plenty of other countries thought that he was too, as well as previous US administrations. During Bill Clinton's presidency, he spoke of the threat posed by Iraq's WMD programme and the potential need for the US to use force to combat it. It is also alleged that Clinton used the CIA to try to get rid of Saddam in two attempted coups in 1995 and 1996.

It seems that there was some information out there that suggested Saddam was up to something. It just turns out that it was almost entirely wrong. There are plenty of examples of this. There were claims that Saddam had developed unmanned aerial vehicles capable of spraying chemical or biological weapons on distant targets. There were other claims that Saddam had made several attempts to buy special aluminium tubes as part of a secret nuclear programme. It was also claimed that Iraqi agents had tried to buy uranium yellowcake from Niger. All of this information turned out to be untrue.

There have been two US government enquiries into how the information presented to the US public was so wrong. I was surprised at how bad the mistakes they found were. They both found that there was very little new evidence on Saddam's WMD programme, since UN weapons inspectors had been forced to leave Iraq in 1998. It was found that the US intelligence community had no human sources since that time with direct access to Saddam's weapons programme, but that it relied on other countries' intelligence services and defectors for its information. It was found that much of the information in recent years came from unreliable sources.

As far as I can see the real question is: how did such flawed intelligence end up being presented to the US public as such a clear case for war? To this question, different sources give different answers.

Both of the US government investigations (the first was a senate select committee and the second was a commission set up by Bush) placed the blame with the US intelligence services – although neither committee investigated the government's role in the issue. They argue that there were mistakes at all levels. The original data was of poor quality and the analysis of it was flawed. In addition, although there were plenty of people who had their doubts about it, or who were in possession of other information that contradicted the general belief that Saddam had WMD, the doubts and contradictory information were not passed on to government policy makers.

Various reasons are put forward as to why this might be. Perhaps the intelligence services, only too aware that they had not managed to prevent the 9/11 attacks, ignored the doubts because they did not dare make another mistake that resulted in harm to US citizens. Also, Saddam had a record of successfully concealing WMD. The US intelligence services had been surprised by the extent of his WMD programme during the First Gulf War, and his behaviour since then seemed to be that of a man who was hiding something. Whatever the reason, the 2002 National Intelligence Estimate that was presented to the government, and from which the Bush administration constructed much of their argument for war, clearly stated that Saddam had WMD. The doubts and contradictions in the argument were relegated to footnotes in the classified version, and were not present at all in the publicly-released version.

Other commentators are not satisfied with this argument and argue that the Bush administration was to blame in the same way that the intelligence community was. After all, there were doubts about the reliability of the information in the footnotes of the national intelligence estimate. And there were enough occasions when various agencies questioned the overall picture of Saddam's WMD. For example, Air Force analysts reckoned that Saddam's unmanned aerial vehicles were for reconnaissance and not for spraying chemical or biological weapons. Outside the US, Hans Blix, head of the UN's weapons inspection team in Iraq stated repeatedly that no evidence that Iraq was developing WMD had been found.

According to this view, the Bush administration chose not to credit the doubts because it had already decided to go to war with Iraq. Various members of the administration had been campaigning for regime change for the past decade. Immediately after the horrific attacks on the Twin Towers, the Pentagon set up a small intelligence cell, called the Office of Special Plans, with the sole purpose of looking for links between Saddam and Al-Qaeda. Apparently, in early 2002 Bush is quoted as saying to Condoleezza Rice: 'Fuck Saddam. We're taking him out.' That does not sound like a man who is in much doubt as to his intentions.

As ever, several reasons are put forward for why the Bush administration was so set on going to war. Maybe they were convinced that Saddam was guilty despite the lack of proper evidence, and felt that they could not risk another 9/11. Donald Rumsfeld, the Secretary of Defence at the time, said that the Bush administration 'did not act in Iraq because we had discovered dramatic new evidence of Iraq's pursuit of weapons of mass murder. We acted because we saw the existing evidence in a new light, through the prism of our experience on September 11th.'

Or maybe, the WMD story was only one reason for the war

with Iraq, and the administration had other hidden ones that it did not wish to make public. Several commentators point out that the neoconservatives and their allies in Bush's government had been keen to attack Iraq for many years. They were looking for an excuse to expand US power in the Middle East region, and they chose WMD as their excuse. As Paul Wolfowitz, Deputy Secretary of Defence at the time and the most prominent neocon in the government, explained the situation: 'For bureaucratic reasons we settled on one issue, weapons of mass destruction, because it was the one reason everyone could agree on.'

If the above view is the correct one, then the Bush administration is guilty of incompetence. It did not have the nous to realise that there were too many mistakes in the intelligence it was given about Saddam's WMD for it to form a valid reason for going to war.

But most experts are happy to go farther than this, and say that the Bush administration purposefully misrepresented the information. They say that it was perfectly aware of the flaws in the case for WMD, but it consciously chose whatever evidence best suited its argument, and ignored everything else. These commentators see the neocons as being the main driving force behind Bush's decisions, whether or not he himself was aware of what they were up to. They allege that the Office of Special Plans, which was set up by Rumsfeld, himself a neocon-sympathiser, to provide an alternative view of intelligence on Iraq to the CIA and other agencies, was only interested in presenting information which agreed with the neocons' preconceived ideas. Some commentators say that the government is guilty of more than just selectively choosing its information – although I would think that that is bad enough. They say that the Bush administration actually put pressure on government agencies to produce information that supported the case for war against Iraq. All through the build-up to the war, top government officials were saying that Saddam definitely had WMD, and these statements put pressure on the

CIA and other agencies to conform. Also, Dick Cheney, the Vice-President and a neocon ally, made constant visits to the CIA, adding to the pressure. Some intelligence professionals have said: 'It was not that they (the intelligence community) were being asked to change their judgments, but that they were being asked again and again to restate their judgments.'

I guess this is one of those issues on which it is difficult to make a judgment. Experts say that it is unlikely that the Bush administration would be so brazen as to present a case if they knew for certain that it would be found to be false. Bush and his colleagues must have been pretty sure that they would find at least some of the weapons that they claimed Saddam had stockpiled, even if they were aware that the available intelligence was not particularly reliable. Once they had made the decision to go to war, it was hard not to dress the available intelligence up to look as convincing as possible. It was especially tempting to indulge in a little window dressing, because there were plenty of other good arguments knocking around for the invasion of Iraq. A democratic pro-US Iraq would strengthen the US position in the Middle East. It would encourage other countries to move in the same direction. It would send a strong message to other Middle Eastern dictators that the US meant business.

'Lying' is probably a bit too strong a word to label what the US government did. It is unlikely that they made anything up. 'Manipulation of the evidence' seems closer to the truth. They were convinced of the need to go to war, and went about constructing an argument for doing so, without much regard for a careful analysis of the information they were given.

Unfortunately for them, not only did it turn out that Saddam had no WMD at all, but their invasion of Iraq and removal of its leader opened up a whole can of worms for which they were totally unprepared.

WHY DID THE USA NOT SIGN THE KYOTO AGREEMENT?

'We will not do anything that harms our economy, because first
things first are the people who live in America.'
George W Bush 2001

Bush's withdrawal of the US from the Kyoto Protocol is often
brought out as proof of his generally destructive outlook on the
planet, but the US government was deeply concerned about the
possibility of internationally enforced caps on their greenhouse
gas emissions from the very start. The general feeling was that
such caps would push up the price of energy in the States, leading
to the loss of jobs and damage to the economy.

For a long time, it was felt that the scientific evidence for
human responsibility for global warming was far too weak to
make emission caps a reasonable option. US politicians felt it was
just too risky to gamble the economy of the nation on a response
to a problem that might not ever materialise. They preferred to
carry on as usual, whilst global warming was investigated further.

As a result of this point of view, the US government spent all
its time trying to avoid signing up for anything definite. George
Bush Snr negotiated successfully at the Earth Summit of 1992 in
Rio de Janiero to prevent binding legislation being passed. He
said: 'It is never easy to stand alone on principle. But sometimes
leadership requires that you do. And now is such a time.'

Bill Clinton committed the US to agreeing a binding target
for its greenhouse gas emissions in 1996, but his actions were

met with anger in the Senate, who were annoyed that they had not been properly consulted. In response, they passed the Byrd-Hagel resolution, which stated that the US should not sign up to any binding treaty unless such a treaty also placed limits on the emissions of developing countries as well. It also stated that the US should not sign such a treaty if it were found to be damaging to its economy. The resolution passed in the Senate by ninety-five votes to none and was supported by both Democrats and Republicans.

Senators had various reasons for supporting the resolutions. Senator Byrd, a senior Democrat, felt that it would be counter-productive for developing countries such as China and India to be allowed to continue to increase their emissions. Manufacturing companies would simply move to countries where there were no limits on their greenhouse gas emissions, so that the economies of developed countries would suffer without there being any overall effect on the problem. Senator Hagel, a Republican, restated the common argument about scientific evidence: 'We shouldn't take any action until we know the consequences...'

Clinton went on to sign the Kyoto Protocol in November 1998, under which the US would pledge to reduce its carbon dioxide emissions by 7% compared to 1990 levels. However, the treaty still needed to be ratified by the Senate in order to become binding. As a result of the strong opposition from senators, Clinton never tried to achieve this.

It was against this background that George Bush Jnr took over as president, and he quickly took measures to distance himself from the Kyoto agreement. In early 2001, he abandoned his campaign pledge to place limits on the carbon dioxide emissions of power plants, and shortly after that he announced bluntly that the US had no intention of ratifying the Kyoto Protocol.

To justify his decision, he gave the same arguments as the US had given before. He stated that, if the US met its Kyoto target, it would result in the loss of 400 billion dollars to the economy, and 4.9 million jobs. Although he accepted that human activity was responsible for global warming, he argued that it was still not clear what the effects of global warming would be. In addition, he said that it did not make sense to sign a treaty which did not also assign targets to countries such as China, which was expected to overtake the US in its greenhouse emissions in the next few decades.

Behind all of this was the US concern that greenhouse gas limits would damage the competitiveness of US goods on the global market. They would not be able to compete with developing countries which would not have to factor the costs of meeting targets into the price of their goods.

Nor was the US just worried about developing countries. Some argued that the US target of 7% was particularly unfair, and would damage its economy in comparison with other developed countries as well. They argued that the US population was growing fast compared to the almost-stable populations of European countries, and that its economy had also grown faster since the 1990 baseline year. As a result, a 7% decrease would be far harder for the US to achieve than the 8% decrease that the EU had agreed to.

Bush emphasised that, although the US was withdrawing from Kyoto, this did not mean that it was not confronting the problem of global warming. In support of this, he cited the amount of money that the US puts into global warming research, separate legislation passed to reduce greenhouse gases and petrol usage, and US membership in the Asia–Pacific Partnership on Clean Development and Climate, an agreement by which countries can impose targets on themselves, but without any enforcement mechanism.

In addition, there has been plenty of activity in the US at state and city level aimed at reducing carbon dioxide emissions. As a state, California ranks as the 12th highest emitter of greenhouse gas emissions in the world. In August 2006, it passed legislation aiming at a 25% reduction in its emissions by 2020. In March 2007, around

400 US cities agreed to work towards meeting the US Kyoto-target, led by Mayor Greg Nickels of Seattle.

In spite of all this, Bush has been strongly criticised by governments and environmental organisations for withdrawing from the Kyoto Protocol. Although the Protocol does have its problems (and may not in fact go far enough towards addressing greenhouse gas emissions), and although many countries look like they will fail to meet their targets in 2012, it remains the only attempt at a legally-binding international treaty to tackle the problems of global warming. By withdrawing, the US undermined the international consensus that the Protocol looked to achieve. Critics of the US argue that the countries of the developed world must take the lead. Only then, will it be possible to persuade developing countries that they too should cooperate.

FURTHER READING

Fukuyama, Francis, *After the Neocons: America at the Crossroads*, London: Profile (2006).

Halper, Stefan and Clarke, Johnathan, *America Alone: The Neo-Conservatives and the Global Order*, Cambridge: Cambridge University Press (2004).

Lindsay, James and Daalder, Ivo H., *America Unbound: The Bush Revolution in Foreign Policy*, Indianapolis: John Wiley and Sons (2005).

Mann, James, *Rise of the Vulcans: The History of Bush's War Cabinet*, London: Viking (2004).

Woodward, Bob, *Plan of Attack: The Road to War*, New York: Simon and Schuster (2004).

http://andrewsullivan.theatlantic.com

http://www.johnpilger.com

THE
DEVELOPING WORLD:
UNFAIR TRADE

WHERE DID THE DEVELOPING WORLD DEBT COME FROM?

'The history of third world debt is the history of a massive siphoning-off by international finance of the resources of the most deprived peoples. This process is designed to perpetuate itself thanks to a diabolical mechanism whereby debt replicates itself on an ever greater scale.'
El Hadje Guissé, UN Sub Commission on Human Rights

Nowadays, you are not meant to talk about 'the developing world' and 'the developed world' – you are meant to talk about the North and the South. Some of you may be wondering if it is OK to talk about the First World and the Third World. Mention those terms in front of a development worker and they will look at you with pity and disgust. You see, both the 'developed–developing' division, and the 'First–Third' division suggest that the countries of the world are in some kind of ranked order, with the wealthy countries at the top, and the poor countries at the bottom. This is, apparently, just the kind of thinking that got us into the current mess in the first place.

In case you are confused, 'the north' is what you would call the developed world, and 'the south' is what you would call the developing world. They are just geographical terms, you see – no judgment attached to them. My problem is that I have a strong belief that, as geographical terms, they should be geographically correct. And Australia, whilst geographically being as south as you can get, is developmentally in 'the north'. Therefore, I am going to ignore them, and stick to 'developed–developing'.

Whilst we are in the area of potential linguistic pitfalls in the world of development, I might as well tell you that you are not meant to talk about 'brainstorming' either. I once asked at a seminar why this might be. The seminar leader looked at me with pity. The term 'brainstorming' is – and it really should be obvious to you – potentially offensive to epileptics, since, as the seminar leader explained to me in the style of a primary-school teacher addressing a two year old, an epileptic fit can feel like a storm in one's brain. The correct terminology is, in fact, 'thought-shower' – although that is almost certain to change in the near future, once it starts triggering off incontinents in development seminars around the world.

Third World, developing world, the south – whatever you choose to call it – there is general agreement that it faces plenty of difficulties, not least of which is its massive debt burden. Currently, according to the Jubilee 2000 'drop the debt' campaign, the world's poorest countries pay around 100 million dollars every day to the world's richest countries. Whilst all countries have debt – and many of the richest countries have much larger debts than this – many of the poorest countries are struggling to cope. For example, Liberia currently has a total debt of 3.7 billion dollars, whilst its annual government budget is 120 million dollars.

But what I don't understand is where all this debt came from in the first place. I understand that the countries of the developing world must have borrowed some money at some point – but how did their debts get so out of control? Wasn't there a limit on their credit card, or something equivalent?

It is possible to trace some countries' problems back to their gaining independence from colonial masters. At this point they found themselves expected to deal with the international economic system despite a lack of education and experience in how to do so. For the most part, the colonial rulers had refused to let the locals get involved in the game whilst they were in power.

It seems a little unfair to have expected them to master the rules as soon as independence was declared. I get the feeling that global economics is a very complicated game indeed.

Even so, everyone was muddling along reasonably well. The developing world took out loans from the developed world to build up their infrastructures and things – but taking out loans for this kind of thing is normal. Countries do it all the time. The US national debt is in the trillions. So nobody could see that it would cause any trouble.

Then came the 1970s. At the beginning of the decade, the OPEC countries put up the price of oil. As a result, they made so much money that they were unable to spend it all, and so it piled up in their accounts in private banks. The private banks were desperate to invest it – apparently it is not good for them to just hold on to cash, although for the life of me I can't understand why. The economic conditions of the time meant that it made sense to lend it to developing countries, who were only too happy to cooperate, since everyone told them it was a good idea.

Borrowing only makes sense if you are going to invest money in something which will make money in the future. Unfortunately, many of the loans did not get used in this way. Governments were keen on prestige projects, which often turned out to be economically unsound. For example, the Philippine government of Ferdinand Marcos borrowed 2.1 billion dollars to build the Bataan nuclear plant. Nothing wrong with a nuclear plant, you might say – a country needs energy sources – but this one was unique in the atomic industry since it is the only one to be built in an active earthquake zone. Given its precarious position, it is probably good that it has never been switched on, but there is no denying that it was a massive waste of money.

Loans were also used to buy weapons – another purchase that was unlikely to give back much on the initial investment. It has been estimated that 20% of the developing world's debt can be attributed to the purchase of arms. Towards the end of the 1980s, the Ethiopian government spent an average of thirteen dollars per head on its military, and seven dollars per head on health and education.

None of this was helped by the prevalence of corruption in many of the governments to which money was loaned. It is alleged that the Philippine official responsible for setting up the Bataan contract, a Mr. Herminio Disini, a golfing partner of President Marcos (I always knew golf was a suspicious game – why would you hit a tiny ball massive distances into a tiny hole if there wasn't something else in it?) received a very sizable chunk of money for his pains, allowing him to set up house in a castle near Vienna.

In the 1980s, Zaire (now the Democratic Republic of the Congo) had a debt of around 5 billion dollars. This turned out to be roughly the amount of money that its president, Mobutu Sese Seko, managed to pocket over the course of his rule. Amongst his possessions, he was able to count eleven chateaux in Belgium, houses in Paris, Nice, Switzerland and the Costa del Sol, and a fleet of planes. Meanwhile, a Zairean teacher was surviving on a salary that only bought a quarter of the food he needed to survive.

Rather oddly, as the result of corruption and the weakness of local currency, much of the money loaned to developing countries ended up going straight back into accounts in the banks which had loaned it, never going anywhere near the general populus.

Despite all this, the international financial system rumbled on without seeming to worry too much. There was a general feeling amongst bankers that you couldn't lose by loaning to a country, since countries, unlike companies, would not be allowed to cease to exist. Some time or other, you would get your money back. Comforted by this thought, they continued to hand out loans.

Unfortunately, towards the end of the 1970s, the international economy conspired against the developing world, in a way that nobody had predicted. First of all, international interest rates went up significantly, and so outstanding debts began to grow at an alarming rate. Simultaneously, the price of oil and manufactured goods went up, whilst the price of raw materials went down. Since most developing countries depended on selling the latter to buy the former, they found themselves with a cash flow problem.

Poor countries found it harder and harder to make the interest payments on their loans. Finally, in 1983, Mexico announced that it was unable to do so. It was followed in this announcement by several other countries. The international finance community panicked. The banks suddenly discovered that they had loaned out more capital to the developing world than they actually had to. They could not afford not to be paid or else there was a real chance that the entire financial system would collapse.

To the bankers' relief, the crisis passed. The leading world powers and financial institutions came together and rescheduled the loans of the struggling countries, often forcing them to adopt specific economic reforms in return. In general, such reforms involved cutting spending on things like health and education, whilst building an economy based around exporting raw products and resources. Critics blame this approach for ongoing poverty in the affected countries.

Even though the financial world might feel that they are out of the woods – as the middle-income debtors, like Mexico, who had taken out the largest loans, are back on track with payments – the problem is far from resolved for the world's poorest countries. For many of these, their total income is far less than the yearly interest they are expected to pay, forcing them to take out more loans just to pay the shortfall. For such countries, it is hard to see any possible means of escape.

SHOULD WE BE IN FAVOUR OF CANCELLING DEVELOPING WORLD DEBT?

'An immediate and vigorous effort is needed, as we look to
the year 2000, to ensure that the greatest possible number of
nations will be able to extricate themselves from a
now intolerable situation.'
Pope John Paul II, New Year address, 1999

With the Pope and Bono on the side of cancellation of developing
world debts, you wouldn't think there'd be any dilemma over
the question of whether or not to support the cause. Rock and
religion are powerful movements with plenty of persuasive facts
at their fingertips: the developing countries have paid off their
original loans many times over, the UK could finance the debt
owed to it if every citizen paid three pounds each year over a
period of ten years and so on.

I think I was repeating these facts to a friend of a friend in a
pub – making out, as you do, that I personally had discovered
them, collected them, and forged them into my very own ground-
breaking argument for debt cancellation. He was a banker, a quiet
one. Bankers don't normally get the same amount of limelight
as Bono, partly because they don't wear sunglasses to make their
opinions seem more mystic. When a banker makes a point, you
suspect it is based on information in the *Financial Times*. When
Bono makes a point, you suspect it is based on divine insider
information. But I had to admit that this banker's points were

good ones:

You can't just let a country off paying its debt. It will undermine the whole financial system. It will encourage other countries to wriggle out of their financial commitments. It will tempt the same countries to take out further loans with no intention of paying them. It will discourage banks and other organisations from giving loans for fear that they will never be paid back. It is deeply unfair on those countries that have scrupulously paid back what they owe. For example, Bangladesh, whilst facing plenty of difficulties, has managed to keep up-to-date with its payments.

Imagine a street of homeowners, all toiling away to pay off their mortgages. Imagine what would happen if the bank suddenly announced that No. 3 and No. 7 were no longer required to make their payments, because they had squandered all their funds on hot tubs and wall-size fish tanks. Not only that, imagine what would happen if the bank then announced that it intended to increase the payment rates for the other houses in order to recoup the money they had lost. There would be plenty of unhappiness.

It is a good point. But Bono – if only he would take his glasses off – does have some counter-arguments at his disposal. First of all, many of the current governments of developing countries had nothing to do with running up the debts that they find themselves saddled with. And there are many cases in which it appears unfair to expect them to take on that debt – especially as they often fought against those who had incurred the debt in the first place.

South Africa, for one, has a good case. Why should the current government service the debts of the apartheid government which they fought so hard to displace? In 1988, the organisation Action for Southern Africa estimated that 28 billion dollars of the region's debt was due to apartheid, and the wars and destabilisation that it caused. This figure was equivalent to three quarters of the region's total debt at the time.

Secondly, Bono can argue that the banks must take some share of the blame for the outstanding debts. In the 1970s, they showed little caution about who they were lending money to. They failed to properly investigate what the money would be used for, or whether they was any likelihood of getting it back, due to a naïve belief that lending to countries was a safe option. In addition, the banks have profited from the situation in a way that is not true of the countries involved. It could also be argued that unless they bear some of the costs of sorting the situation out they are likely to make similarly risky loans in the future.

Finally, it seems unreasonable to argue that if countries are released from their debts they may be encouraged to run up further debts. Many of the indebted countries have already suffered significantly in their attempts to keep up with their interest payments. They have been forced by the World Bank and the International Monetary Fund to make radical changes in their economy, which in many cases has resulted in the neglect of public services and the consequent suffering of the general population. It is unlikely that they will want to go through this experience again.

So it appears that Bono, for the most part, wins the day. It does seem unfair to place the burden of debt repayment solely on the shoulders of the developing world. But the banker's arguments must be taken into account as well. There must be very good reasons for granting the reduction of debts, or there will be repercussions in the global finance system. In fact, countries are keen not to default on their debts because they are aware that it might endanger their chances of getting future credit from lending institutions.

Recent developments have moved some way towards accepting that responsibility for the debt must be shared. The Heavily Indebted Poor Countries scheme, set up by the World Bank and the IMF, grants countries cancellation of some of their debts if they fulfil a strict economic plan. To qualify, a country must have a debt burden that is one and a half times its export earnings. But critics say that this scheme still fails to share responsibility for the debt crisis between the developed world and the developing world, that it places too many damaging economic restrictions on the poor countries involved, and that it does not go far enough in assisting them. In addition, there are plenty of countries that remain outside HIPC which have equally pressing needs.

It seems Bono still has a job to do.

ARE WE MEETING THE MILLENNIUM DEVELOPMENT GOALS?

'On current trends, most Millennium Development Goals will not be met by most countries.'
Global Monitoring Report 2004, World Bank.

Every now and then, it seems, a group of the world's leaders get together, shake hands, make speeches, and set some targets. It is front page news for a while – but soon the meeting is over and the leaders go their separate ways. The targets slip from the headlines to the inside pages. Then they quietly slip into oblivion.

In September 2000, the member states of the United Nations adopted the Millennium Convention and declared their commitment to global development. After consultation with many international organisations, the Millennium Development Goals (MDGs) were put forward as the measure by which this commitment should be measured. The Goals are a series of specific targets in eight development areas aimed at improving the living standards of the world population. The UN list the goals as follows:

- Eradicate extreme poverty and hunger
- Achieve universal primary education for all
- Promote gender equality and empower women
- Reduce child mortality
- Improve maternal health
- Combat HIV/AIDS, malaria and other diseases

- Ensure environmental sustainability
- Develop a global partnership for development

So taking the first MDG – 'eradicate extreme poverty and hunger' – as an example, the targets are to halve the proportion of people who live on less than a dollar a day, and to halve the proportion of people suffering from hunger. The deadline for this and the other targets is 2015.

I'm afraid that I was not particularly excited when the Millennium Development Goals were first announced. Targets are such dull things and they rarely appear to have any value at all. Governments so regularly fail to meet their own targets that you are left wondering why they bothered to announce them in the first place. Or even worse, a government announces that it has succeeded in meeting a target, only for its opposition to attack the legitimacy of its claim. It is no wonder that politics loses its appeal when it is reduced to two indignant parties throwing numbers at one another.

The citizens of countries in the developing world don't share my lack of enthusiasm. In Rwanda the government prepared its own development manifesto, called Vision 2020. It was a set of targets that the country gave itself which broadly agreed with the Millennium Development Goals. In the capital city of Kigali it is common to find all sorts of things bearing the name 'Vision 2020' – from minibus-taxis, to grocery stores to hair salons. For Rwandans, Vision 2020 and the Millennium Development Goals promised a real change to their quality of life and gave hope for a better future.

So it is really worrying to find that, as things stand, these promises are going to be broken. According to a Global Monitoring report from the World Bank in 2006, many developing countries are still off track, despite some individual success stories. In Africa, many countries have experienced no improvement in their levels of poverty. Only 34 developing countries out of 143 are on track to halving their numbers of underweight children. Ten million children under the age of five still die each year of easily preventable diseases.

It makes depressing reading. Still, the report argues that there is time to turn things around. It makes several recommendations, which are pretty similar to those found in previous reports. It asks for a fairer international trading system with an end to the tariffs and subsidies that prevent developing countries from earning foreign capital. It asks for better government with more accountability and transparency. It asks for an increase in aid and a better use of it by its managers.

I have a sinking feeling about these targets. Some criticise them for being too demanding in the first place, but others criticise the wealthy countries for a lack of real commitment to achieving them. The World Bank, which is responsible for the global monitoring reports, states that an extra forty to seventy billion dollars in aid are needed each year in order to meet the targets. Its 2004 report stated that of the 170 million dollars committed to a global fund for education, only six million had been stumped up. That doesn't look to me like a sign of commitment.

More fundamentally, many experts suggest that the Millennium Development Goals are an example of flawed thinking from the start. Firstly, they ignore the issue of governance. Throwing money at the problems of the developing world will have little effect, if the governments of developing countries do not operate effectively. And secondly, it makes no sense for the international community to come up with universal targets in this way. Each developing country has its own issues, and each developing country should tackle these issues as it sees fit.

WHAT DOES THE FAIRTRADE LABEL MEAN?

'I pity the man who wants a coat so cheap that the man or woman who produces the cloth will starve in the process.'
Benjamin Harrison, 23rd President of the United States

'Before you've finished your breakfast this morning,
you'll have relied on half the world'.
Martin Luther King

Nowadays, most food in the supermarket seems to have some kind of label stuck on it to indicate that it is better than your average product. It is a banana's equivalent of wearing Gucci sunglasses. Some foods wear the 'organic' label. Others prefer 'local'. Yet more and more foods are only seen in 'Fairtrade'.

It occurred to me the other day, as I politely refused a plastic bag, that I had very little understanding of what these different labels meant. I am sometimes quite happy to pick up a couple of designer products off the shelves, drop them in the basket, pay a higher price at the check-out, and wander off into the world with a vague sense that I have contributed to the intellectual and emotional well-being of chicken-kind. At other times, having got out of a different side of the bed, I operate in a different mindset, scrupulously avoiding the labels. I treasure my callousness, as I consign some other chickens somewhere or other to a lifetime of cramped captivity. I mean, do I really want my life choices to be influenced by poultry? I have a sneaking suspicion that when society breaks down, it will be the people who worry about the chickens that perish first.

Whatever my position *vis-à-vis* chickens, I decided that I wanted to know a bit more about what fair trade actually meant, especially as the fair trade market is growing all the time. There was a 40% increase in sales from 2005 to 2006 and Fairtrade products account for a significant proportion of sales in their various product categories in Europe and the USA. Most of these sales are in foodstuffs, but the variety of products available from fair trade sources is expanding. You can buy Fairtrade roses, Fairtrade footballs – there are even rumours that you'll soon be able to buy Fairtrade condoms. I can already imagine the advertising campaign: 'TWICE THE SATISFACTION.'

For a product to carry the Fairtrade mark, it needs to have been purchased directly from the producer under set conditions. These conditions vary in detail from product to product, but stick to certain underlying principles. Firstly, to take one example, Fairtrade coffee farmers must be paid a price that covers their production costs and their cost of living. These living costs include enough money to buy food for the family, pay hospital fees and send their children to school. In recent years, due to the low international price of coffee, non-Fairtrade small coffee farmers have struggled to survive.

Secondly, producers are paid a small amount in addition to this basic price. This extra sum is to be used to help them develop their farms and communities. A study of the cooperative Coocafe in Costa Rica (lots of 'C's in that sentence) found that farmers had used this money in various ways. They had set up scholarships to enable promising students to attend university, they had organised training programmes to encourage the cultivation of organic coffee and they had started an environmental programme to protect local communities of turtles.

There is more to Fairtrade, however, than just paying a higher price. When exporters sign a Fairtrade agreement, they must agree to pay a certain percentage of the price up front, if the farmers wish. This allows farmers to access funds year-round, and helps them plan their farming activities more productively. The exporters must also commit to long-term contracts. This gives farmers further security. Also, by building a relationship between the farmers and their customers, it allows the farmers to gain information and understanding about how the international market for their product works.

Finally, the Fairtrade mark guarantees that certain basic rights are upheld at all levels of the supply chain – from the farmers, to the exporters, to the shops. It guarantees that employees have the right to form unions, and that women's and children's rights are observed. Fairtrade also encourages sustainable farming and respect for the environment, although these are not necessarily part of Fairtrade contracts.

IS FAIR TRADE A GOOD THING?

'A well-intentioned, interventionist scheme...doomed to end in
failure.' Brink Lindsey, Cato Institute Senior

When it comes to 'good causes', I have a habit of digging my
heels in. I don't like the passive role of being asked to give. I don't
like the heartfelt pleas of actors on the television – mostly because
I know that, in most cases, they are good at acting heartfelt pleas. I
don't like the endless pictures of poverty and suffering.

I am always surprised by my reaction. It is a hard one to gauge
– but I think it is made up of a mixture of guilt, helplessness
and ignorance. I know that life has dealt me a good hand. I am
confused by the multitude of problems in the world and I am
aware that I don't know enough to make an informed decision
concerning what to do about them.

Above all, if I am going to hand over some money, I want to
know that it is going to be used productively. I want to know that
the problem it is trying to solve is a real one. I want to know that
it is not going to end up in the pockets of administrators, who
spend their time relaxing by swimming pools with cocktails at
sunset.

For these reasons, and despite the fact that the principles of fair
trade all seem like worthy goals, I viewed fair trade with suspicion.
I wasn't convinced that it could all be good news. The fair trade
movement is not without its critics. Many claim that it either
has little effect, or even that it possibly does more harm than
good. They argue that fair trade gets in the way of the operation

of a free trade market, which, if left to itself, would bring about exactly the kind of improvements that fair traders want.

So, for example, critics object to the way that the fair trade movement persuades small coffee farmers to continue growing coffee, even though there is currently a world surplus of it. The allegation is that fair trade is therefore encouraging uneconomical farming, and, whilst it may bail some farmers out in the short term, it will not be sustainable in the long run. The low price of coffee is considered to be a signal to these farmers from the free market that they must either move to the cultivation of specialist coffees (for which the market is currently growing) or to some other crop altogether.

If these critics are correct, then fair trade is essentially no different from direct aid. The higher price paid to the producer is basically a gift to them from their wealthy customers in the developed world – and, according to the above argument, it is not a gift that they are using wisely. The customer in the supermarket would be better off saving their money by buying non fair trade products and donating the surplus cash to an organisation with a proven track record in development.

There are some powerful counter-arguments though. On a practical level, it is very difficult for poor farmers to simply shift to another crop. Coffee plants take several years to develop, for example. If a farmer decides to grow another crop, he will lose several years of investment and hard work. He will also probably need to get his hands on some capital to get his new venture started. This is simply not an option for most poor farmers. They can't afford to lose their investment and they have no access to funds.

Fair traders argue that the extra money and help that fair trade makes available to farmers does exactly the opposite of tying them into an inefficient crop. It allows them to develop their farms and diversify into other markets. For example, the Costa Rican Coocafe collective now produces several types of coffee bean, including organic coffees, as well as plantain chips. Fair trade, they argue, allows farmers to escape their dependency on standard coffee.

But more than this, fair traders argue that the current trading market is not at all 'free'. It is loaded against small farmers in the developing world who do not have easy access to the market, or to credit, or to information – a situation which is assumed to be the case in a properly 'free' market.

To give an example, a cocoa farmer in West Africa is unlikely to have his own transport. He probably has to rely on a man-with-a-truck to come and take his produce to market. Since this man-with-a-truck probably has no competitors, he has total power over the price he gives for the cocoa. Unsurprisingly, the cocoa farmer tends to get a pretty poor deal. Not only that, it is probably the same man-with-a-truck who provides him with loans and market information. In Central America, these men-with-trucks are called 'coyotes', because of their unscrupulous way of dealing with their suppliers. Fair trade, with its insistence on a proper price, prevents this kind of exploitation from occurring.

Fair trade also demands that certain standards are met within a 'free' market. It argues that it is not OK for workers to work in dangerous and unhealthy conditions, or for children to be forced into employment at the expense of their education – even if such practices lead to a product with a cheaper price. By purchasing a fair trade product, a customer is lending their support to this view.

Fair traders can also argue that it does not make sense to claim that fair trade gets in the way of the free market. Nobody is making the customers purchase fair trade products. The producers won't get paid if there is no market for what they grow. Rather, the label 'Fairtrade' can be seen to be a new brand in the market, for which customers are prepared to pay a higher price. As it has turned out, the brand is a popular one, which fair trade farmers are keen to take advantage of.

By buying into the 'Fairtrade' brand, customers are showing

their support for a fairer 'free market'. They are giving poor farmers access to a system from which they have normally been excluded, and they are supporting the right of these farmers to have a reasonable quality of life. Importantly, as the fair trade market has grown, it has affected the mainstream trading system. Supermarkets and international business have been keen to identify themselves as 'fair traders' – although there is much debate about whether this is really the case.

Fair traders admit that it is possible that fair trade will have to change in the future. It hasn't been around long enough for its impacts to be properly measured. But they argue that there is plenty of anecdotal evidence that it is bringing considerable benefits to many farmers around the world, and, perhaps more importantly, its existence provides a visible and fairly high profile criticism of the current trade system, which is in many respects decidedly unfair.

I have to say that I find these arguments quite convincing. And I like the fact that it isn't just a gift – I am exchanging money for goods. As far as I am concerned, this feels much more natural than the act of simply sending a cheque to a charity. So, when it comes to fair trade, I might stop digging my heels in.

WHAT CAN BE SO BAD ABOUT A
BUNCH OF BANANAS?

'Goods produced under conditions which do not meet
a rudimentary standard of decency should be regarded
as contraband and not allowed to pollute the channels of
international commerce.'
Frankin D Roosevelt, May 24th 1937

I am not a large fan of the banana myself – something to do with
the way their flesh glistens when you bite into them – but it seems
such a simple fruit. I couldn't see how banana cultivation could
cause much offence to anyone. It turns out that the banana *is* a
simple fruit. Or rather the banana that makes it to the supermarkets
of the developed world is. Whilst there are hundreds of different
types of banana, the vast majority of exported bananas are all of
one type: the Cavendish. The Cavendish might sound like the
kind of banana you would find in a gentleman's club relaxing
after a game of tennis with a brandy and a pipe, but in reality it
is one of the most important export products in the world. The
banana is the single most profitable item in UK supermarkets.

For this reason, people take it very seriously. The Cavendish is
big business. It gave rise to the 'banana republics' of Central and
South America. To this day, Ecuador, Costa Rica and Colombia are
amongst the largest banana exporters in the world. So important
is the Cavendish that it has led to armed conflict. In 1954, the
elected government of Guatemala was toppled in a military coup
in which the CIA played a part. It is alleged that the US United

Fruit Company, who owned massive banana plantations in the country, encouraged their government to get involved for fear that the new government would force them to sell some of their land back to Guatemalan peasants.

There have been plenty of worrying stories in recent years about the cultivation of the Cavendish. *The Ecologist* magazine reports that, on many plantations, working conditions are terrible. It found that Guatemalan banana workers commonly work twelve-hour days, often for less than the legal minimum wage of their country. Many workers are unable to complain about such issues, because they are not allowed to organise into unions. There are plenty of accounts of workers who have been fired for trying to do so.

Because plantations only grow one strain of banana, they rely heavily on the use of pesticides to protect their crop. As a result, plantation bananas need the most chemical treatment of any crop, except for cotton. In many cases, workers are expected to apply these chemicals by hand to the bananas, often without any protective clothing. Planes spray the plantations, whilst people continue to work amongst them. The *New Internationalist* reports that these chemicals cause sickness amongst the workers. There are allegations that they lead to deformed fingers and joints, and that 15,000 male workers in Costa Rica are sterile as a result of exposure to them.

It is not just the workers that suffer as a result of intensive banana cultivation, but also the environment. The chemicals lead to pollution, and the disturbance of local ecosystems. In Central America, populations of turtles and sea cows are threatened, and offshore coral reefs are being destroyed. New banana plantations in West Africa are being planted at the expense of local forest. The intensive methods of banana farming lead to soil erosion and destroy soil fertility.

I have to say that I was surprised at the severity and number of all these allegations. I had always had a fairly idealistic vision of bananas hanging from trees in a jungle somewhere – probably fuelled by repeated childhood viewing of the animated film *The Jungle Book*. In future, I will try to be less naïve.

HOW DOES INDIA MANAGE TO MANUFACTURE SUCH CHEAP HIV/AIDS DRUGS?

'Fifty percent of people with Aids in the developing world
depend on generic drugs from India.'
Ellen't Hoen, Medecins Sans Frontieres

I used to think the answer to this question was to do with cheap labour, but in fact it's all about patents.

Once, when I was at school, I created an innovative squash ball warmer. It was so innovative that it actually reduced the squash ball to liquid rubber. If the world had felt ready for such an item, I would have considered applying for a patent. A patent prevents anyone else from copying the product for which the patent has been issued. In other words, if I had applied for a patent and if my application had been successful then nobody else would have been allowed to manufacture my squash ball warmer. As it turned out, there was not enough commercial interest for me to pursue this course.

In the 1970s the Indian government stopped issuing patents for drugs. As a result, its drug producers could happily make copies of drugs (or 'generic drugs') which were under patent in other countries. Generic drugs were cheaper to make, because no money had to be spent in order to develop them. India quickly became the major player in the world market for generic drugs. Nowadays, the international medical and humanitarian aid organisation Medecins Sans Frontieres (MSF) estimates that

India produces over half of the medicines currently used for the treatment of AIDS in developing countries.

However, India's status has come under threat. In 1995, the international agreement on Trade-Related Aspects of Intellectual Property Rights (or TRIPS) came into force. The World Trade Organisation has since put strong pressure on member countries to change their laws to bring them into line with this agreement which puts forward a common set of rules for intellectual property rights, including rules on patents. In 2005 India introduced its new patenting laws in line with TRIPS. The WTO agreed that drugs patented in their original country of manufacture before the TRIPS agreement were exempt, so India can carry on making copies of these drugs. But any company that has produced or patented new drugs since 1995 is now able to apply for a patent in India as well. If the Indian government issues a patent for a particular drug, then Indian drug producers cannot produce copies of it.

This has caused something of a hullabaloo. Organisations like MSF are worried that the new laws will threaten the supply of cheap drugs for the treatment of AIDS and other diseases in the developing world. It is not so much of a problem for the standard first-choice drugs. India can continue to produce these because they initially came on to the market before 1995. In fact, even the international drug companies now produce these cheaply for poor countries.

The concerns of MSF and other organisations lie with new drugs. Drug companies will produce more effective treatments that under the new patenting laws others will not be able to copy. Also, as the HIV virus becomes resistant to the standard treatments, HIV-infected individuals will need access to different 'second-line' drugs, and these too will be unavailable in a generic form. According to the AIDS charity AVERT, it currently costs 277 dollars per year to treat an HIV patient in Cameroon using the standard 'first-line' drugs, and 4,673 dollars per year using 'second-line' alternatives.

There is currently a high profile case being fought between the Indian government and the drugs company Novartis. In its new patent laws, the Indian government has ruled that it will only issue patents for drugs that are genuinely original – rather than for small changes in pre-existing drugs. It has refused to issue a patent for Novartis's new cancer drug on the grounds that it is really only a minor development of a previous product – one which Indian drug producers can copy. Novartis is fighting this judgement. Campaigners worry that if Novartis wins the case, there will be a long queue of other companies lining up to get patents for their slightly-altered products.

There are mechanisms by which developing countries can get their hands on essential drugs. If a drug is not available to them, or if it is too expensive, a country can issue a compulsory license. They are then allowed to break the patent on the drug and manufacture it themselves. At the end of 2005, the Brazilian government persuaded the drug company Abbott to drop the price of one of its drugs by threatening to issue a compulsory licence. The Thai government recently issued several of them.

Still, compulsory licences are a complicated business, and in many cases developing countries are fearful of angering the large drug companies – and the countries where they are based – by breaking patents and copying their drugs. In response to the Thai government's issuing of compulsory licences, Abbott refused to sell any of its newer products in Thailand. Smaller countries are unlikely to dare to take on such important global players.

It is also possible for drugs companies to issue voluntary licenses, in which they allow other companies to produce their drugs. A few years ago, GlaxoSmithKline allowed the South African company Aspen to produce copies of three of its drugs free of charge, as long as Aspen promised to contribute 30% of its sales to NGOs fighting HIV and AIDS in South Africa.

It is also possible that the fears of MSF are unfounded. Some commentators say that the new patenting laws will not necessarily make future drugs more expensive for the developing world. They argue that the large drug companies, as a result of competition with the producers of generic drugs and of growing international pressure, have accepted the need for two markets for their drugs. They charge high prices to customers in the developed world so that they can cover the costs of the research and development work that goes into producing new drugs, whilst charging lower prices for essential drugs in the developing world. Even if the competition from generic drugs is removed, the commentators say there is enough international pressure to make sure that they stick to this state of affairs.

At this point in time, it seems to be a matter of wait-and-see.

HOW DO WE KNOW IF NGOS ARE
DOING A GOOD JOB?

'Almost anything that one can say about [NGOs] is true – or
false – in at least some instance, somewhere...'
Esman, M. & Uphoff, N. in *Local Organizations: Intermediaries in
Rural Development* (1984)

I spent a couple of years as a teacher in a secondary school in
Rwanda. The school I taught at had a link with a school in
Australia, which occasionally raised funds for it. During my time,
this link resulted in two improvements. A group of Australian
schoolchildren visited and painted the school hall yellow, and
twenty laptop computers arrived on the back of a truck.

I don't want to be ungrateful, but it struck me that there might
have been better uses for the raised funds than yellow paint and
computers. The school hall had been a little dingy, but it was
perfectly capable of doing its job, and was really only used by the
karate club anyway. Meanwhile, the students slept two-to-a-bed
in the dormitories (not out of choice), and most of the classroom
windows were broken. And what about the computers? Well, I
know that ICT is meant to be the solution to most problems,
but it can't do much if there is no regular electricity supply. Nor
is it that helpful if nobody knows how to use it. The computers
sat around in a room, to which visitors of the school were often
shown. But students never went near it.

I know that the link between the two schools was an informal
one, and that NGOs are meant to be far more professional

about how they use their funds, but I get the feeling that there is a general concern that NGOs might not offer good value for money. For example, when people look at some of the countries in Africa into which millions of dollars of aid have been poured, it doesn't seem as though the money has had much obvious effect. So I tried to find out if there is any research on this question, and whether it is possible to check on an NGO's track record.

I discovered that there were plenty of academics and development professionals who were asking the same question. Many people had become concerned about the efficacy of NGO work in the wake of the Rwandan genocide of 1994. In many cases, the NGO-run refugee camps at the time ended up as safe havens for those who carried out the genocide. These people used them as an arena to exert power over the real refugees, and it was felt that NGOs did very little to prevent this situation.

First things first. It is not true that NGOs waste much of the money they are given on their own administrative systems. According to a survey of the top 500 fundraising charities, 84% of the funds received were spent on charitable work. The question is whether this money is put to good use. Those Australian laptops didn't really make that much difference.

In recent years, there has been an increase in studies that try to measure the impact of NGOs. The findings of these studies have been mixed. I read one report that looked at four different NGOs in Bangladesh and India. One of them had managed to set up a network of schools and micro-credit schemes, support local fishermen in a successful campaign against large trawlers, and encourage women to prosecute men who illegally took more than one wife. Another had poured around two million pounds into schools and health services, nearly all of which had been forced to close.

There has recently been extensive research into the NGO response to the tsunami disaster in 2004, in which 227,000 people died and 1.7 million people were forced from their homes. There was a huge worldwide response to this catastrophe. In fact, more money was given than was actually needed. Again, the findings of this research were mixed. On the positive side, the Tsunami Evaluation Coalition found that NGOs were successful in providing good emergency relief in the immediate aftermath of the tsunami, and in quickly helping the affected areas to move towards recovery. Within six months, schools and health facilities had been restored, often in better condition than before the disaster, and 500,000 people had a fixed roof over their heads. It was estimated that 70% of Sri Lankan households in the affected areas had a steady income. Tourism was on the rebound.

On the negative side, the TEC found that there was often poor coordination between the NGOs and poor communication with the local people, so that inappropriate and, sometimes unwanted aid was given. Some NGOs had so much money to use, and were under so much pressure from the media to achieve immediate results, that bad decisions were made.

So, it is clear that there are high-quality NGOs out there, and also that there are low quality ones. I would like to know how to find out which of these categories a particular NGO is in. Unfortunately, that is where the problem lies. Despite increasing interest in this question, there is still not enough research to help us make such judgments. NGOs publish information about themselves, and, since the introduction of the Freedom of Information Act in the UK, it is also possible to access all government information in the area. But it is difficult for a non-NGO person to make sense of such data, and there is certainly no recognised independent body to which we can turn to help us out – although there are currently one or two movements that aim to set up something like a standards committee for NGOs..

The difficulty lies in how you judge an NGO's performance. The Union of International Associations in Brussels lists 58,000 non-profit organisations, with 42,000 different strategies on 4,800 categories of issues. Unsurprisingly, it is impossible to come up with one benchmark against which to judge such a variety of groups. In addition, the impact of an NGO's work can be very hard to measure. For example, whilst it is definitely a success that local fishermen have managed to prevent illegal trawling in their waters, it is not easy to measure how much of a success it is, or to compare it with other success stories.

So, for the moment, it is difficult to decide how we should determine the efficacy of a particular NGO. Still, the good news is that there is plenty of work being done in this area. Donors want to know that their money is being put to good use. NGOs themselves are keener than anyone to establish a proper evaluation system. They recognise that assessment can help them improve the services they provide, and make better use of their limited funds. As a result, they have begun to voluntarily set up monitoring systems.

It seems that some of the largest NGOs have already begun to make significant changes in the way they work. For example, Oxfam is increasingly leaving on-the-ground tasks to local groups so that it can focus on lobbying around issues of trade and development. ActionAid has decentralised and moved its headquarters to South Africa in order to be closer to the people it works with. Hopefully, as NGOs improve their monitoring systems more information about the impact of their work will become available to you and me.

FURTHER READING

Allen, Tim and Thomas, Alan, *Poverty and Development,* Oxford: Oxford University Press (2000).

Easterly, William, *The White Man's Burden: Why the West's Efforts to Aid the Rest Have done So Much Ill and So Little Good*, Oxford: Oxford University Press (2006).

Forsyth, Tim (ed.) *The Encyclopedia of International Development*, London: Routledge (2004).

Sachs, Jeffrey *The End of Poverty: How We Can Make It Happen In*

Our Lifetime, London: Penguin (2005).
Willis, Katie *Theories and Practices of Development,* London:
Routledge (2005).
http://www.takingitglobal.org
http://youthink.worldbank.org
http://www.yesweb.org

THE ENVIRONMENT: TROUBLE IN THE GREENHOUSE

IS IT POSSIBLE THAT GLOBAL WARMING IS NOT TAKING PLACE?

'There is still time to avoid very large-scale climatic shifts, and the very much worse effects of them, but time is running out.'
Tony Juniper, Friends of the Earth

Global warming is confusing for most of us, because it lies in the realm of Science. I stopped trying to understand science many years ago, but I retain a healthy distrust of its findings for very good reason. Every school science experiment that I ever carried out always came up with the exact opposite result to the one it should have.

Despite my lack of confidence, there seems little doubt that the world is warming up. There may be arguments in the scientific world about exactly why this might be, but there is near unanimous agreement that it is the truth. There are a variety of different pieces of evidence for it, the most important of which are historical records of temperature around the world.

Ferdinand II, the Grand Duke of Tuscany, invented the first thermometer in the 1660s and shortly afterwards temperature readings were being taken all over Europe and the US. It was just over 20°C in Philadelphia on July 4th 1776 – the day the Declaration of Independence was signed. Thomas Jefferson took the reading.

Before long, temperature readings were being used to help predict local weather and by the 1900s, there were all sorts of weather-predicting associations spread over the world. In 1951, the World Meteorological Organisation was set up in order to encourage all this information to be shared, so that more accurate forecasting could be achieved. Nowadays we have grown used to overly-cheerful smartly-dressed men and women strolling across a map of our country telling us what the weather will be like over the next few days.

It is only in more recent years (since the 1970s in fact) that scientists began to try and use all this information to look at global temperatures over the last century. There are all sorts of complications involved. An official thermometer, like a student at an old-fashioned boarding school, must satisfy strict rules. It must be situated at a certain height above the ground and be kept in a well-ventilated white box. Ideally, it should remain at the same location during its lifetime.

Also, some parts of the planet have far less data. There are hardly any weather stations in the southern hemisphere compared to the northern hemisphere and there are no weather stations on the planet's oceans. Over the years, ships have recorded the temperature of the sea surface. They used to just dunk a bucket in the water. Nowadays, the process is a bit more scientific. Scientists have to take the method used to check the sea's temperature into account, because it has an effect on the readings.

However, despite all the finickitiness of the process, the various major centres for monitoring global temperature are in broad agreement of the results. The surface temperature of the planet has warmed by between 0.4°C and 0.8°C since the late 19th century, and a significant part of this warming has taken place in the last twenty or so years.

There are other indicators that the earth is warming up. For the last few decades, weather balloons and satellites have been measuring the temperature of the part of the atmosphere near to the earth's surface (known as the troposphere). There has been considerable controversy over these readings (which initially suggested that no warming was taking place), but, as corrections have been made to take account of various inaccuracies, these readings too have indicated a rise in temperature.

On top of that, there is no doubt that glaciers are retreating, and snow and ice cover have diminished. Montana's Glacier National Park expects to have lost all its ice by 2030, and the Arctic sea ice has lost half its thickness since 1950. Trees and plants are blooming earlier, and some insect and bird species are moving northwards. Inuits report that unknown birds are arriving in the Arctic regions. Other species are struggling to survive in the changing environment.

It is not just the temperature. It is possible that other aspects of the climate system are changing as well. Rain patterns appear to have altered – droughts and violent rainstorms seem to be on the increase. It is also suggested that there are more clouds around than before.

All these different measures of the world's temperature agree. The planet is getting hotter. Not only that but the warming process seems to be on the increase, and it is this that is particularly worrying scientists. 1998 was the hottest year globally since records began, and places two to six are filled by the first five years of the new millennium.

IS IT POSSIBLE THAT HUMANS ARE NOT RESPONSIBLE FOR GLOBAL WARMING?

'Is it only terrorists that we're worried about? Is that the only threat that is worth our attention?' We are witnessing a collision between our civilization and the Earth.'

Al Gore

A while ago, I watched Al Gore's *An Inconvenient Truth*. He is a dependable-looking man and he stood in front of some sizeable graphs. I couldn't see any flaws in his arguments linking human greenhouse gas emissions to the current rise in temperature. Right, I thought to myself, there is no escaping it – human global warming is a fact, and we should do something about it.

But then, just as I was about to make some radical lifestyle changes, I came across a documentary in which a group of intelligent-looking scientists – most of them sitting in book-lined studies to emphasise the point – argued that humans were not to blame, and that the recent rise in global temperature was due to an increase in solar activity. They had their own set of sizeable graphs to back up their argument.

Well, what is a concerned non-scientist to do? I began to have nightmares in which I was imprisoned in a room without exits, decorated with graphs of all shapes and sizes. In order to escape I had to understand the significance of these graphs, but each one seemed to mean something different. I was trapped forever.

Or maybe not. It is true that there is still plenty of argument in scientific circles about the global climate and how it functions. It is a very complicated subject, and new discoveries are being made all the time. However, despite these arguments, the scientific community is in broad agreement about the general picture.

The global climate has gone through all sorts of changes over the lifetime of the Earth. Throughout the last 10,000 years, something called 'the Dansgaard–Oeschger cycle' has triggered cold periods. One of these may have put paid to the Old Kingdom in Egypt. Most recently, the Little Ice Age (around 1200 – 1650 AD) may have polished off the Norse colonies on Greenland. In contrast, when dinosaurs were around (between 250 million and 65 million years ago), global temperature was roughly 5°C warmer than nowadays. During this period, it was warm enough for animals and plants to thrive in polar regions, whilst vast deserts covered other parts of the planet.

There are all sorts of factors involved in the global climate, including the output of energy from the sun, the Earth's orbit, natural levels of greenhouse gases, volcanoes and asteroids. The eruption of Mount Pinatubo in the Philippines in 1991 cooled the earth's climate for several years, because the particles it sent into the atmosphere cut the amount of sunlight able to reach the planet's surface. It is thought that an asteroid collided with Mexico 65 million years ago. The heat it produced caused such widespread fires that global temperature rose and half of the planet's species died. More recently, human activity has complicated the picture by adding more greenhouse gases to the atmosphere, as well as other forms of pollution.

Some greenhouse gases, like carbon dioxide, methane and nitrous oxide are present in the Earth's atmosphere naturally. In the last 200 years, however, human beings have been responsible for releasing additional amounts of these gases into the atmosphere, as well as throwing some gases of their own invention into the mix for good measure. Chlorofluorocarbons (CFCs) are an example of man-made greenhouse gases. They have been used in aerosols, foam manufacture, air conditioning and refrigeration, although their production has declined drastically in recent years because of their effect on the ozone layer.

Because Nature is clever, there are natural processes which remove greenhouse gases from the atmosphere, such as plant photosynthesis, which removes carbon dioxide. The problem is that these processes are unable to keep up with the rate at which man is now producing the gases.

Scientists know that carbon dioxide, and other greenhouse gases, have an important effect on global climate by studying records of the climate in the past (which they have reconstructed by a variety of methods). At the end of the last ice age, the temperature warmed up by 6°C in 4,000 years (a very short time in the world of climate change), during which sea levels rose by 120 metres, atmospheric carbon dioxide rose by a factor of 1.3, and atmospheric methane (another powerful greenhouse gas) doubled. It is suspected that the high temperatures of the dinosaur age were a result of carbon dioxide released by underwater volcanoes, and that the gradual cooling of the Earth over the past fifty million years or so may be the result of a decrease in atmospheric carbon dioxide (although causes of this are uncertain).

Any combination of factors may be responsible for a change in climate. In addition, the factors do not operate independently of one another, but are in a state of constant interaction. So what scientists have done is to create complicated models of the global climate, which include all of these factors and their relations with one another. Current models contain programmes which simulate the climate of the atmosphere, the land surface, and the oceans, and the way these climates interact. They are able to model the way that these climates are affected by the Earth's orbit and other natural events as well as by man-made greenhouse gases and other pollutants.

These models are not perfect. Scientists are constantly updating them in the light of new discoveries about how the global climate works. At the moment there is plenty of debate about how to model cloud cover and about the interactions between the different layers of water in the oceans. Despite these simplifications, these models do a very good job of reconstructing the planet's climate, especially the last hundred years or so.

Sceptics often like to point out that the temperature change over the last century is not consistent with the theory of man-made global warming. They say that a good portion of the warming happened in the first half of the century, before greenhouse gas emissions had really kicked in, and that, from around 1940 to around 1970, just when you would expect the global temperature to rise quickly, it actually dropped. Only since the 1970s has the temperature begun to rise rapidly again.

Scientists can reply, using their models, that the temperature of the last century cannot be explained by looking at only one factor. Changes in solar output contributed to the warming at the start of the century, and the cooling in the middle of it. Pollution from industry, in the form of airborne particles, which peaked during the middle of the century also contributed to the cooling period. Meanwhile, greenhouse gas concentrations in the atmosphere were constantly on the increase and this too had an effect.

Global temperature in the 20th century cannot be explained by natural causes alone, nor can it be explained by looking at only man-made effects. Only when both natural and man-made factors are considered do the models fully reproduce the patterns of the last century. The most sophisticated of these models can go on to reproduce the global climate for thousands of years before this as well.

So, the models are pretty precise. They contain a very good approximation of the mechanisms that lie behind global climate. When it comes to the last twenty years or so, the models show that the major factor in the rise in temperature is our addition of greenhouse gases to the atmosphere. None of the other factors can account for the rapid pace of the temperature increase.

Over the years, there has been plenty of disagreement amongst scientists about the details of the global warming story outlined above, allowing controversial documentaries to be made. However, the Intergovernmental Panel on Climate Change (IPCC), the international scientific body set up to analyse the question of global warming, has gradually become more and more adamant that human emissions are responsible for the rise in temperature.

In its Second Assessment Report, published in 1995, it stated: 'The balance of evidence suggests a discernible human influence on global climate.' In its Third Assessment Report, published in 2001, it stated: 'There is new and stronger evidence to suggest that most of the warming observed over the last fifty years is attributable to human activities.'

In a report produced in preparation for the release of the Fourth Assessment Report later this year, it stated: 'The understanding of anthropogenic warming and cooling influences on climate has improved since the Third Assessment Report, leading to very high confidence that the globally averaged net effect of human activities since 1750 has been one of warming.' In this context, 'very high confidence' means that the scientists on the IPCC are more than 90% certain that humans are the cause of global warming. That is good enough for me.

WHAT EXACTLY IS THE KYOTO PROTOCOL?

The entry into force of Kyoto is the biggest step forward in
environmental politics and law we have ever seen.'
Jennifer Morgan, director of the World Wide Fund for Nature
(WWF) conservation group's climate change programme.

The Kyoto Protocol is probably the most well-known agreement
on the environmental scene. It has an austere ring to it. I imagine
that it was negotiated with great decorum over endless rounds of
tea served in delicate Japanese teacups. But precisely what was it
that was agreed?

The United Nations Framework Convention on Climate
Change (UNFCCC) was presented at the Earth Summit held
in Rio de Janeiro in 1992. Around 150 countries signed up to
it, pledging to take steps to reduce their emission of greenhouse
gases, which were blamed for global warming. The signatories of
the framework only committed themselves to voluntary actions,
but it paved the way for annual international meetings to discuss
these issues, and to negotiate binding targets for the reduction of
greenhouse gas emissions.

At the third of these international meetings, in Kyoto in
December 1997, the Kyoto Protocol to the UNFCCC was
adopted. The protocol was a legally-binding pledge to reduce the
emission of six 'greenhouse gases' (the most important of which
was carbon dioxide) in thirty-eight developed countries to 5.2%
below 1990 levels by the period 2008–12.

The protocol made a distinction between developed countries and developing countries. Under the protocol, only developed countries were given targets, in recognition that they were the main contributors to the problem, and that it was unfair to hinder developing countries from further development at this stage. However, developing countries were able to sign and ratify the treaty.

Each developed country was able to negotiate its own individual emissions target, depending on its particular circumstances. For example, the EU negotiated that its target was 8% below 1990 emissions levels, whilst Russia simply had to maintain its 1990 levels and Australia was allowed to increase its emission by 8% from its 1990 levels. There was plenty of controversy over these individual targets and not all developed countries went on to commit themselves to the Kyoto Protocol, most notably the US and Australia.

A country has a number of options for meeting its particular target. It can make use of various technologies that prevent pollutants being released into the atmosphere, or it can try to reduce its emissions by improving the efficiency of its industry.

In this context, the Japanese government came up with an interesting approach to the problem, suggesting that Japanese office workers should wear fewer clothes. As Tokyo and other Japanese cities are so very hot all office buildings and bars are heavily air-conditioned. The government argued that, if workers left their jackets and ties at home, the air-conditioning would not need to be turned up so high and valuable energy would be saved. Government ministers were ordered to set a good example and get rid of their suits, while the environment minister even offered to put on a fashion show to demonstrate suitable outfits.

Under the Protocol, if a country does not think it can meet its target by straightforward emissions-reducing measures, there are alternatives. It can develop 'sinks' which use natural processes to take greenhouse gases out of the atmosphere. For example, a country can plant trees, which remove carbon dioxide from the air.

Another option is for the country to take part in the Clean Development Mechanism (CDM), a scheme set up by the protocol. The idea behind this is that there is an opportunity now to encourage developing countries to develop in a way that will avoid the production of high levels of greenhouse gas emissions in the future. Developed countries can fund projects in such countries, and gain credits which they can offset against their own deficit. For example, Germany could sponsor the building of a wind farm in China, and it would receive an allowance that it could use to meet its own target.

Lastly, a country can become involved in carbon trading schemes. There are several of these schemes in existence, the largest of which is the European Union Emissions Trading Scheme (EUETS). In such schemes, countries that think they are going to exceed their targets can buy credits from countries that think they are going to meet their targets. The idea is that this will provide a financial incentive to countries to reduce their emissions.

As part of the protocol, the sinister-sounding Compliance Committee was set up to monitor whether or not countries were meeting their targets. If the even more sinister-sounding enforcement branch of this committee decides that a country has failed to meet its targets, then that country must make up 30% more than this deficit by the next review date. Until the country has done this, it is not allowed to take part in any of the emissions trading schemes.

The impact of the Kyoto Protocol is a matter of controversy. There are plenty of arguments against its effectiveness. At this stage, it seems that the majority of countries that committed to it are going to miss their targets. For example, the European Environment Agency reported in 2004 that eleven of the fourteen EU countries are on course to overshoot their allowances.

In addition, it is a problem that several of the world's largest sources of greenhouse gases are not required to meet targets. The US did not commit to the Protocol, and China and India were given no targets to meet due to their status as developing countries. Also, there is a danger that manufacturers will simply move their operations to countries where no emissions caps are in place. Currently though, it is the developed world we need to worry about. The developing world is much more efficient in its expansion of production and energy use.

Finally, even if all the countries bound by the protocol met their targets, some scientists argue that this reduction will not have a significant impact on global warming, or at least nor for a period of several decades.

However, supporters of the protocol argue that it is an achievement just to have negotiated such an agreement between so many of the world's nations, and that it will provide an important step towards the implementation of further climate agreements in the future. They say that if countries do not begin to make changes now, then it will be all the more difficult for them to adapt in the future.

IS CARBON TRADING EFFECTIVE?

'We've been involved in transactions in China, and have caused
to be reduced, at very low cost, the equivalent of Sweden's total
annual output of greenhouse gases from across its economy.'
James Cameron, vice chairman of Climate Change Capital (an
investment bank that specialises in low emissions businesses)

The idea of trading in pollution sounds a little bizarre. I can understand the concept of going to work to buy and sell tea or gold – but putting on a suit to trade in greenhouse gases? That's crazy talk.

Or maybe not. In the 1990s, the US successfully set up a sulphur-trading scheme for its industries in order to cut down on levels of atmospheric sulphur dioxide – the gas which causes acid rain. This scheme managed to cut sulphur dioxide emissions in the US to about a half of their 1990 levels at a fairly low cost to industry. Its success is a major reason why many countries want to take the same approach towards other environmental problems.

The Kyoto Protocol put forward carbon trading as one of the methods by which countries could encourage their industries to meet their targets for greenhouse gas emissions.

Under carbon-trading, a country (or a region) breaks down its overall emissions allowance into individual allowances for its industrial companies. It then issues credits to each company, allowing each one to produce emissions up to this individual allowance. If an industry is unable to meet its individual target, it must purchase further credits from other companies. If an industry manages to produce less emissions than its individual target, it is able to sell them and make a profit.

Currently, the largest carbon trading scheme is the European Union Emissions Trading Scheme (EU ETS), which was launched at the start of 2005. It covers 12,000 industrial installations, which between them are responsible for around 50% of the EU's carbon dioxide emissions.

In the first phase of the EU ETS, which ran from 2005 to 2007, the scheme only dealt with carbon dioxide emissions, but in its second phase, which will run from 2008 to 2012, it will cover all greenhouse gases, and expand its remit to industries that were originally not subject to the scheme, such as the aviation industry.

There is no doubt that there have been problems with the first stage of the EU ETS, which has produced mixed results. On the positive side, the EU has managed to set up the structure of the scheme and the trading system with very few problems – an impressive achievement for such a complicated project.

On the negative side, it has handed out too many credits to their companies, so that, in many cases, companies did not have to make any changes in their practices in order to meet their emissions targets. As a result, nobody was interested in buying the credits, and their price collapsed (at one point, by as much as 60% of their original value). This fall in price further contributed to the problem, as the few companies that were unable to meet their targets were simply able to purchase cheap credits rather than deal with the source of the pollution.

There has been heavy criticism over the fact that some of the biggest polluters involved in the EU ETS were actually able to make huge profits by selling many of their credits, because the emissions targets they were set were too lax. Analysts say that UK firms collectively earned 940 million pounds during the first phase by selling excess credits.

However, in many ways, the first phase of the scheme was only ever really meant to be a trial run. It is the second phase, which will make or break the EU ETS. It is vital that the EU ensures that it allocates the correct amount of allowances. Encouragingly, it looks like the EU is being much stricter with its member countries this time around.

Each country must come up with a National Allocation Plan, which sets out how many credits it thinks it needs. In the first phase, the majority of countries pushed for over generous allowances, most of which were granted. This time they are trying the same thing, but the EU has not played along. So far, all the plans have been cut back – except that of the UK.

At the moment, the jury is out over carbon trading schemes. It sounds like a good idea in principal. Supporters say that carbon trading allows far greater flexibility in how companies tackle the reduction of their emissions, and encourages them to innovate in order to make money by beating their targets. They say that trading schemes manage to bring together environmentalists and businessmen in a way that other approaches to the problem do not. They agree that the EU ETS has had its problems, but they say that it is important to support it, because only then will other countries consider getting involved.

On the other hand, opponents of carbon trading say that it gives polluting businesses too much influence over the process. They say that the problems in the first phase of the EU ETS show that it is impossible to prevent big businesses from manipulating such schemes for their own benefit. They say that emissions trading is a largely untried system, and that we do not have the time to wait around and see if it works. They argue that it is better to rely on government regulation, which has been used effectively to deal with such issues in the past.

Despite the arguments, it looks as if carbon trading is here to stay. There are plans to link up the EU scheme with a Californian version, and other regions of the world are thinking about setting up their own schemes.

Some authorities are going much further, and suggesting the formation of a global carbon trading market. Let's hope it all works out.

WHAT IS AN ECOLOGICAL FOOTPRINT?

'Eventually, the world will no longer be divided by the
ideologies of 'left' and 'right', but by those who accept
ecological limits and those who don't.'
Wolfgang Sachs, Wuppertal Institute

In its 2006 Living Planet Report, the WWF (that is the
World Wildlife Fund, NOT the World Wrestling Foundation,
although arguably both protect endangered species) calculated
the ecological footprint of an average Norwegian. It turned out
to be 5.8 global hectares.

I don't have any problems with the concept of an average
Norwegian. I know that he/she is tall, blond, and silent, with
a love for nudity and Abba, and a hankering for seaborne raids
on neighbouring countries. It is the 'ecological footprint' about
which I am unsure. What is one of those?

According to the WWF, the average Norwegian footprint of
5.8 hectares is made up of several parts: 0.8 hectares is cropland
(to produce food, animal feed, fibre and oil), 0.2 hectares is
grazing land (to provide animals for meat, hides, wool and milk),
0.9 hectares is forests (to provide wood, wood fibres, pulp and
fuelwood), 0.2 hectares is fishing ground (to provide fish and
seafood, 0.3 hectares is built-up land (for housing) and 3.3 hectares
is land required to absorb CO_2 emissions from fossil fuels.

The WWF arrived at these figures by calculating an estimate
of, for example, how much food, animal feed, fibre and oil the

average Norwegian consumes, and then, using global averages for how much cropland is needed to provide these goods, it calculated an estimate for how much cropland the average Norwegian needs to keep himself supplied with these items. The estimate, in this case, was 0.8 global hectares. A global hectare, therefore, is not any existing piece of land, but a conceptual piece of land that produces on a world average.

The WWF arrived at the other figures for the average Norwegian in a similar way. Since humans do not just affect their landscape through the consumption of products, but also leave behind waste, the WWF considered CO_2 emissions in its calculations, estimating how much land would be needed to absorb the CO_2 emissions of the average Norwegian. As you can see, it is by far the largest component of the Norwegian ecological footprint

The WWF made similar calculations for many other countries. The three countries with the highest ecological footprints are the United Arab Emirates (11.9 global hectares), the USA (9.5 gha), and Finland (7.6 gha), and the three countries with the lowest ecological footprints are Afghanistan (0.1 gha), Somalia (0.3 gha), and Bangladesh (0.4 gha).

There are plenty of other methods for calculating an ecological footprint, and it is possible to calculate one for any kind of community or for any individual. From all the averages floating around in such calculations, you can see that an ecological footprint is never going to be a precise measure, but it does begin to give an idea of just how much demand humans (in the developed world anyway) are placing on their environment.

The WWF calculates that, if the world was shared out equally amongst the current human population, then each person would have roughly 1.9 global hectares to provide for all their needs and absorb all their wastes. As the world population increases, this figure will grow smaller. Pretty much every country in the developed world has ecological footprints that are above this figure, and most of them by a considerable margin. To give you an idea of the problem, the ecological footprint for London is roughly 90% of the land area in the UK.

Since the 1980s, the ecological footprint of the average human being has exceeded 1.9 global hectares. Currently, the human population requires about 25% more land for its needs than the planet can supply in a sustainable manner. It is estimated that, on current trends, by 2050 we will need two Earths to support our way of life. According to academics, it is possible for humans to exist like this for a short period of time, by using up the planet's resources quicker than they can be replaced. In other words, for a while, we can get away with cutting down all the planet's forests, catching all the planet's fish and pumping CO_2 into the atmosphere. However, we will very quickly reach a point where we damage the environment irreversibly, creating problems for our own continued survival.

If we want to improve this situation, the main issue is our CO_2 emissions, which we will need to significantly reduce. It seems that action is beginning to be taken on this issue through the Kyoto Protocol and other mechanisms, but whether such action goes far enough remains to be seen.

The WWF report shows that developed countries must take steps to reduce their ecological footprints, if their citizens are to live sustainable lives. At the same time, developing countries must be encouraged to develop in a way that improves their standard of living without increasing their ecological footprints. In an ideal world, all countries would enjoy a high standard of living, whilst having sustainable ecological footprints. According to the WWF, the only country that currently manages to meet both criteria is Cuba.

It is all very well for me to be criticising the average Norwegian citizen for their large ecological footprint, but it occurred to me that I should put myself on the line. So, I worked out my own personal ecological footprint using a few of the eco-calculators on the web. It took me longer than expected due to the time spent on complex calculations such as how many kilometres I travel by bus each year. I persevered, though, eventually discovering that there are 3.9 virtual global hectares with my name on them. Or, to put it another way, if everyone in the world lived as I do, we would need 2.4 Earths to cater to our needs.

The eco-calculator was not content with just making me feel guilty. It also had some advice to give on how I could cut down on my demands on the planet. I learnt that a regularly-serviced car has approximately 5% better fuel efficiency, and that a car driven at 70 mph uses 25% more fuel than a car driven at 50 mph. I learnt that energy-efficient bulbs use a quarter of the electricity that a normal bulb uses, and that they last eight times longer. And I learnt that leaving the television on stand-by costs you almost as much as watching it.

There was additional not-so-helpful advice. Apparently, washing-up can be an enjoyable family activity. I beg to differ – I have never felt anything close to pleasure when pulling on a pair of marigolds. Another tip was that it makes sense to use waste water from the bath in the garden, because 'sometimes' bubble bath acts as both a mild pesticide and as a fertilizer. I wonder if 'at other times' bubble bath has the same constructive effect on foliage as napalm?

WHAT IS AN ECO-CITY?

'Dongtan is breathtaking in scale and ambition[...]it is a beacon to
the world on how to achieve a low-carbon future.'

Ken Livingston

It seems that everyone wants to move into the city. For the first
time in human existence, there are more city slickers than country
folk, and it is predicted that by 2050 three-quarters of us will be
living in town. In 1800, London was the only city in the world
with over a million inhabitants. By 1990, there were over thirty-
five cities with more than five million inhabitants.

Even before becoming so densely populated, cities have
always had their problems. In the middle of the 19th century,
for example, Londoners struggled with the smog, sewage and
industrial pollution of their environment. In 1858, the stench
from the River Thames was so bad that debates in the Houses of
Parliament had to be postponed. London was forced to build a
sewage system that could deal properly with its waste.

However, the massive increase in city populations and the building
of many new cities in the developing world pose an entirely new set
of problems. As a result, academics and administrators are beginning
to look at ways to improve how cities function.

In this context, an 'eco-city' refers to an idealised city, which has
been designed so that it has healthy relationships both internally
amongst its citizens, and externally with its region and the global
community. Key issues in the design of such a city are its food
production, its management of waste, its energy production, its

transport system and its accommodation. For an 'eco-city', the emphasis in all these areas is self-sufficiency and efficiency. The idea is that, wherever possible, a city will produce everything it needs to function by itself. In addition, thought must also be given to how to ensure that the city functions smoothly on a social level.

The best example of what this all means is given by the most ambitious project in the area at the moment: China's attempt, in partnership with the design firm Arup, to build a brand-new 'eco-city', called Dongtan, on an island at the mouth of the river Yangtze. Arup is the civil engineering company responsible for the Sydney Opera House, the Pompidou Centre and Tate Modern. Construction of Dongtan starts in 2007, and the aim is that, by 2050, the city will have approximately 500,000 inhabitants.

As a result of its rapid economic growth, China's cities are struggling with smog, sewage and CO_2 emissions. The developers of Dongtan hope to show that further economic growth is possible without adding to the current problems. The experiment is particularly important because China plans to build around 400 new cities in the course of the next twenty years, and because it hopes to show the rest of the world that the theories and systems behind 'eco-cities' can be a practical reality.

Dongtan aims to be totally self-sufficient in electricity and heat. It will have its own heat and power plant, fuelled by rice husks; a waste product from local mills. It will also make use of energy from wind farms and from biogas produced by solid waste and sewage. Individual buildings will have photovoltaic cells and tiny wind turbines to make use of solar power and wind power. At the same time, efficient building design will reduce the amount of energy required.

The transport system will be organised so that nobody will be more than seven minutes away from access to public transport, which will be provided by buses and water-taxis. There will be a network of trails for pedestrians and bicycles. Visitors to the city will have to park their cars outside and enter using public transport.

All the city's waste will be recycled so that there is no need for landfill sites. Organic waste will be used to produce energy, and human sewage will be processed and used for compost in the surrounding farmlands.

There will also be an educational programme to help inform the citizens of the city about how they can contribute to the quality of their environment, and sociologists will be involved in the project with the aim of creating a harmonious community.

If all of this works out, you can see that the city will have limited need to import products from the outside world. As a result, it will not have to make use of the inefficient transport and power supply systems that current cities depend on. Nor, due to its use of recycling and clean fuels, will the city leave behind problems for itself or for the global environment. This is the ideal of the 'eco-city'.

Of course, the world is not a perfect place and so for the most part we will have to make do with the cities we have got. It is rare that there is a chance to build a city from scratch – unless you spend most of your time in cyberspace. However, there are plenty of attempts in progress to improve the functioning of the cities that we live in now, and to move them step-by-step towards the 'eco-city' ideal.

Take London for example. It has introduced the congestion charge to cut down on the use of private polluting vehicles in central areas and worked on improving its public transport system. There are plans to centralise waste management, so that more waste can be recycled rather than dumped, and there is a push towards making far greater use of renewable energies. Several small-scale developments exist in the city that are starting to put into practice the ideas that lie behind the 'eco-city'. For example, the Beddington Zero Energy Development (BedZED) in South London produces its energy from a small on-site power station which runs on off-cuts from the wood chippings produced during the trimming of the city's trees.

WHAT IS BIOMASS?

'The only source of liquid transportation fuels to
replace oil is biomass.'
Nathanael Greene, author of the 'Growing Energy' report.
(see www.harvestcleanenergy.org)

It is amazing how easy it is to accept a term without question, as
long as it sounds scientific. During my research on the eco-city
of Dongtan, I asked the press officer of Arup how the city would
generate its power. She replied that the main source of energy
would be a power station that used biomass as its fuel. I found
myself nodding wisely at the telephone receiver. 'Ah biomass, what
a sensible and environmental choice that is,' said a voice in my head.
Since this voice seemed to have so much knowledge, I asked it
what biomass actually is. It had absolutely no idea.

It turns out that biomass is a collective term for all living (or
recently living) plant and animal material. So it can be flowers in
the garden, fish in the sea, or a dead squirrel on the road. Humans
have been making use of biomass for years and years. We have used
it as fuel, or to make chemicals and materials, or as food for ourselves
and our animals. There is nothing new about any of this.

It is the use of biomass to produce fuel that has got people
excited in recent years. Each year plant biomass captures roughly
eight times the amount of energy used by humans. So it would be
handy if we could make use of some of it, especially as we tend to
leave plenty lying around in the form of rubbish or crop waste.

In addition, the use of biomass as fuel is not considered to contribute to global warming. When it is burned, it does release carbon dioxide, but it is the same carbon dioxide that it has absorbed over its lifetime from the atmosphere through photosynthesis. So, as long as we replant each crop of biomass, there is no overall disruption of the amount of carbon dioxide in the atmosphere. In contrast, although fossil fuels were originally biomass, they have been hidden away for so long, that, when they release carbon dioxide on burning, it does cause disruption.

Again, the idea of burning biomass for fuel is not a new one. Burning wood was the main source of energy all over the world until the mid-1800s, and in many places it still is. However, it does make sense to make use of waste from agriculture and other areas, rather than just throwing it away.

There are other approaches to the use of biomass as a fuel, though. Various crops (like corn and sugar cane) can be fermented to produce liquid fuels, such as ethanol. In 1975, Brazil introduced the National Alcohol Programme. It was not a government initiative to prevent drink-driving. In fact, it was a drive to reduce the amount of petrol used by motorists. Brazil has the largest sugar-cane crop in the world, and used it to produce both pure ethanol fuels and fuels made from a mixture of gasoline and ethanol. Nowadays, both types of fuel can be bought in the majority of Brazilian petrol stations. Greater use of ethanol reduces our dependence on fossil fuels. It also produces far fewer pollutants and breaks down quickly into harmless components if spilled.

There is a problem with using biomass for fuel in this way, though. You need plenty of land to produce enough raw material. In Brazil, this has already led to deforestation, with all the problems that that entails. If the world were to switch from fossil fuels to liquid biofuels to power its cars, there would be no land left for growing food.

Finally, when biomass is left lying around so that bacteria can break it down in the absence of oxygen, it produces biogas. This is a process that goes on all over the place – from the Arctic tundra to our digestive systems. Biogas is a mixture of methane and carbon dioxide, and it can be collected, for example from landfills, and used as a fuel. In India, villagers fill airtight pits with cow dung, and use the gas produced for cooking. The residue left in the pit can be used as a fertiliser. A major advantage to using biogas is that it prevents methane, which is a greenhouse gas, from escaping into the atmosphere.

WHAT IS THE PROBLEM WITH PLASTIC BAGS?

'In 2001 there was 1,678,900 tonnes of plastic packaging
in the waste stream.'
Department for Environmental Food and Rural Affairs

The polythene bag has been described as 'humanity's worst invention' – which is saying something when you consider it is up against atom bombs and puffer jackets. It nearly didn't get invented at all. Polythene was first discovered by accident in the 1930s by two scientists in Cheshire. When they tried to repeat their experiment, it blew up. They left well alone, but two years later another scientist accidentally reproduced the same conditions because of a leak in his equipment. And they say chemistry is an exact science.

It took another forty years before humans started to mass-produce plastic bags, but once they started they went in for it in a big way. Nowadays, one million new plastic bags are distributed worldwide every minute. The strange thing is that most plastic bags do not need to exist. There is absolutely no reason why I need to collect five new ones every time I go to the supermarket, storing them in an ever-increasing bundle beneath the sink in the kitchen. I know that I am unlikely to make use of them again, but guilt prevents me from throwing them in the bin.

It is alleged that they are a way for supermarkets to create a little more advertising space, and – since the bags are made out of by-products from the fuel production process – for fuel companies to make a little more money.

The problem is that the bags do not decompose quickly. According to some estimates, they may take anything up to a thousand years to break down (although nobody is sure of the exact amount of time, because they haven't been around that long yet). In the meantime, plastic bags sit around in landfills or drift around as rubbish, fragmenting into tiny balls of plastic which pollute waterways and land, and which are swallowed by animals and fish. In 2002, a dead Minke whale washed up on the coast of Normandy. Its stomach contained 800 kg of plastic bags and packaging, including two supermarket bags from the UK. It is no use switching to paper bags. They are just as unnecessary as the plastic kind, and, although they do decompose quickly, they require four times as much energy to produce, generate fifty times as many water pollutants and take up more landfill space.

Some shops have started to make use of degradable plastic bags, which contain an additive that causes them to break down. These bags are certainly preferable to standard plastic bags, but they still require energy to produce, and release greenhouse gases when they decompose.

Recycling is not an easy option either. Recycling rates for plastic bags are currently very low and even if they were to improve, recycling plastics is complicated and expensive, due to the many different types of plastic in use.

Unbelievably, many plastic bags are made in China, shipped 5,000 miles for use in the UK, then sent back to China to be recycled. One particular village in southern China, Mai, even has an area known as 'Plastic Street', which is lined with plastic recycling factories.

It seems that by far the best approach is simply to buy a sturdy bag, and use it for all shopping trips. Several governments around the world have encouraged this practice. The Irish introduced a plastic bag tax of 15 cents per bag in 2002, as a result of which demand for plastic shopping bags dropped by 90% within a matter of months. The Kingdom of Bhutan, which has recently opened up its borders to tourism, has also banned the bags, viewing them as a symbol of the Westernisation it wishes to avoid. Other casualties of its anti-Westernisation policy are tobacco, advertising hoardings and TV wrestling.

IS THERE ANYTHING WRONG WITH DISPOSABLE NAPPIES?

'We believe that people should be free to choose
whatever nappy suits them.'
Environment Agency, UK

Arguments concerning the environmental impact of disposable nappies can be intense and often turn nasty. There are plenty of people out there who have a strong dislike for disposables, and they are ready to make all sorts of accusations against them, none of which have much evidence to support them. Disposable nappies have been variously accused of causing asthma in mice, changing the sexual orientation of whelks and raising the scrotal temperature of baby boys to unhealthy temperatures.

The New Zealand Green Party is not content with simply spreading unpleasant rumours about disposable nappies, it advocates more positive actions as well. It suggests the establishment of 'nappucino' mornings, where parents sip frothy coffee whilst demonstrating how to change cloth nappies. For its most militant members, it suggests dumping fifty-two bin bags full of rubbish in a public place (to symbolise the amount of disposable nappies a household uses in a year), taking a photograph (preferably with a minor celebrity and a baby sitting on a neat pile of twenty cloth nappies also in shot) and sending it off to the local newspaper.

But after the transsexual whelks have gone home, and after the press cameras have stopped rolling, what is the truth about the environmental impact of disposable nappies? How do they compare with reusable nappies? Because there is no doubt that nappies are necessary: a baby has an average of 2.3 bowel movements a day.

In 2005, The Environment Agency in the UK put together a report on exactly this issue. It compared the use of disposable nappies with the use of reusable nappies, for the entire 2½ year nappy-wearing period of a baby's life. It looked at various environmental impacts, such as acid rain, global warming, and the use of fossil fuels. It found that there was little overall difference between which type of nappy was used. Whether you use disposable or reusables, with respect to its nappies, one baby has the same effect on the environment as driving a car for approximately 1500 miles.

The EA goes on to say that the two types of nappy create these impacts in different parts of their life-cycles. For disposable nappies, most of the environmental impact arises during the manufacturing process and during their management as waste after their use, whilst for reusable nappies, most of the environmental impact is the result of the washing and drying process. Using a washing machine and dryer to clean reusables is roughly as bad for the environment as making a disposable nappy from scratch.

The EA report is one of the most comprehensive to date, but already it has come in for a fair amount of criticism. Firstly, it does not tackle the issue of landfill, and the simple fact that, in many countries, we are running out of space for our rubbish. Disposable nappies take between 200 and 500 years to break down, and they make up roughly 2% of all household waste. Nappy companies have developed degradable and recyclable nappies to try and get around this problem.

Secondly, a nappy user (parent, not baby) can cut down on the environmental impact of reusables fairly easily. They can use electricity from a renewable source, they can wash nappies at a lower temperature (apparently 60°C does the job just as well as

90°C), they can make sure that they only wash a full load, and they can dry nappies on a washing line rather than in a dryer. As a result, it is possible to reduce the global warming effect of reusable nappies by a substantial amount with minimal effort.

In contrast, a nappy user (parent, not baby) has no way of reducing the environmental impact of disposable nappies, because these all happen either before or after they have got their hands on them.

Finally, the EA has also failed to investigate thoroughly the issue of the psychological trauma suffered by unwilling gender-swapping whelks. How do you put a price on that?

FURTHER READING

Henson, Robert, *The Rough Guide to Climate Change*, London: Rough Guide Ltd (2006).

Hillman, Mayer, *How We Can Save The Planet*, London: Penguin (2004).

Monbiot, George, *Heat: How we Can Stop the Planet Burning*, London, Penguin (2007).

Porritt, Johnathan, *Capitalism as if the World Matters*, London: Earthscan Ltd (2005).

http://www.realclimate.org

http://www.ipcc.ch

http://www.hm-treasury.gov.uk/independent_reviews/stern_review_economics_climate_change/sternreview_index.cfm

ISRAEL AND PALESTINE: ROAD MAPS AND WRONG TURNS

WHAT IS ZIONISM?

'The bride is beautiful but she is married to another man.'
Viennese rabbis on the possibility of Palestine being a
homeland for the Jews, from *The Iron Wall* by Avi Shlaim (2001)

I had always assumed that 'Zionist' is simply another label for 'Jewish', and so I was surprised the other day to read about an anti-Zionist Jewish group, called Neturei Karta. In the article, a member of this group described how he refused to take an Israeli passport or pay Israeli taxes, even though he had lived in Israel all of his life, because he did not believe that the Jews should establish their own country until the coming of the Messiah. As a result, I realised that 'Zionism' was not simply about being Jewish. What was it about then?

Zion is a biblical name for Jerusalem and Zionism is the belief that there should be a homeland for the Jews. It is not a new belief. Ever since the Roman suppression of Jewish revolts in the first couple of centuries AD, the Jews had been exiled from their spiritual homeland. In fact, many of them had left ancient Palestine even before these calamities. From this time on, the vast majority of Jews lived in communities scattered all over the world. They continued to revere Jerusalem and its sacred places, and their prayers often expressed the desire to return – but for a long period of time no practical steps were taken towards this goal.

It was only in the 19th century that people began to talk about the real possibility of a Jewish homeland. Many Jews were unhappy with their status as outsiders and minorities in the countries that they had adopted as home, especially since anti-Semitism was on the rise. In addition, at this time nationalism was a new and popular idea and all sorts of people were demanding their own homeland – the Jews didn't see why they should be any different.

Certain Jewish thinkers began to suggest that the Jews should take some practical steps in this direction. For example, in 1881, a group of Russian Jews, calling themselves the 'Lovers of Zion', began to actively promote Jewish immigration to Palestine, in reaction to aggression towards Jews in Russia. The term 'Zionism' itself was coined by a Viennese Jewish writer in 1885.

However, the father of modern Zionism is normally agreed to be a man called Theodor Herzl. In the 1890s, he worked as the Paris correspondent for a Viennese newspaper, during which time he was troubled by the strong current of anti-Semitism that he found in France. He came to the conclusion that there was only one solution to the difficulties that the Jews faced in the various countries in which they lived – they must set up their own country.

He may not have been the first to have come up with this idea, but he was the first to give it credibility and a high profile. In 1896, he published his thoughts in a book, called *The Jewish State* and, in 1897, he convened the First Zionist Congress in Switzerland. From this time on, until his death in 1904, he was the leader of Zionism, working hard to gain international support for his ideas.

In the early days of the movement, it was not clear that the Jewish homeland would necessarily be in Palestine. Herzl himself suggested that it could be founded in the empty spaces of Argentina. The British government suggested that it might be less controversial if it was founded in East Africa. However, it soon became clear that Zionist hearts were set on reclaiming a place in their holy land.

Not all Jews supported Zionism. At the time, it was a highly controversial movement. Herzl originally wanted to stage the First Zionist Congress in Munich, but the German Union of Rabbis refused to allow it, arguing that the plan to establish a Jewish state went against the teachings of religious sources and that Jews should concentrate on working for the good of their adopted countries. Left-wing Jews said that the Jews should worry less about their own nation, and more about the problems of all oppressed peoples throughout the world.

Still, the project went ahead over the following decades, both in terms of Jewish emigration to Palestine, and gaining international support. By the start of the First World War, 35,000 Jews had settled in Palestine, and Jews owned 2% of Palestinian land. By the start of the Second World War, there were 467,000 Jews – around a third of the Palestinian population – and Jews owned 15% of the land. The Zionists had also gained qualified support from Britain and the USA for the idea of a Jewish homeland. When the horrifying truth about the holocaust became know, popular opinion united behind them.

Over this period of time, there was still considerable disagreement amongst Zionists about their goals. The mainstream view was a practical one. It was voiced by David Ben-Gurion, who was to become Israel's first prime minister in 1948. He and his supporters first and foremost wanted their own country. Depending on the political climate, they were flexible about its borders – at times they were happy to accept something smaller than modern-day Israel, at times they pushed for the whole of British-controlled Palestine. Initially, they hoped that force would not be necessary to achieve this aim – although this view changed as Palestinian Arab hostility grew to their presence in the area.

The main opposition to Ben-Gurion came from Ze'ev Jabotinsky and the Revisionist Zionists. They felt that the Jews were entitled to the whole of British-controlled Palestine, and they made no bones about the fact that it would only be possible to take control of it after a fight.

After Israel's declaration of independence in 1948, and the ensuing war, the state of Israel consisted of the majority of what had been British-controlled Palestine – but Jordan took control of the lands on the West Bank of the River Jordan, and Egypt occupied the Gaza Strip. The nature of where Israel's 'true' boundaries lie remains contentious to this day.

To give just one example, in November 1995 the Israeli prime minister, Yitzhak Rabin, was shot dead by the right-wing Zionist, Yigal Amir, just as it seemed he was about to bring peace to the region in a deal that was supported by the majority of the Israeli population.

Amir remained unrepentant about the killing throughout the following trial. In his view, Rabin was a traitor to the Jewish cause, because he was willing to return West Bank territory that Israel had occupied after the Six Day War in 1967 to the Palestinian Arabs. For Amir, and others that thought like him, this territory was Israel's by right, and anyone who considered surrendering it was an enemy of the Jewish people.

WHO DREW UP THE BORDERS OF ISRAEL?

'His Majesty's Government view with favour the establishment in Palestine of a National Home for the Jewish people, and will use their best endeavours to facilitate the achievement of this object, it being clearly understood that nothing shall be done which may prejudice the civil and religious rights of existing non-Jewish communities in Palestine, or the rights and political status enjoyed by Jews in any other country.'

Arthur Balfour, Foreign Secretary, November 2nd 1917

In Douglas Adam's bestselling novel, *The Hitchhiker's Guide to the Galaxy*, a character called Slartibartfast is responsible for the geographic design of Norway. He specialised in coastlines, and won awards for his complicated use of fjords. He was irritated to find himself assigned to the coastline of Africa after this, because its lack of glaciers meant that he had no excuse for designing more fjords. He didn't think a coastline was worth much without fjords – they gave it a baroque feel.

If only the colonial powers had put as much thought into their plans for the Middle East after the First World War perhaps some of today's difficulties could have been avoided. Instead, they carved it up with little consideration for the consequences of their actions. Palestine – which at the time included all of what we now call Israel, the occupied territories and Jordan – ended up as a British mandate. (From 1922 onwards, Jordan, or Transjordan as it was called, was administered separately.) The vague idea was that the British would govern Palestine, whilst they worked out how to make it a viably independent country. It turned out that this was easier said than done.

In the lead-up to the Second World War, there was a large influx of Jews into the area. Due to the rise of Zionism and an increase in persecution, particularly under Fascist governments, they wanted to return to their spiritual homeland. The problem was that they didn't necessarily have a very positive attitude towards the Arabs already in residence, and the Arabs were not overly pleased to see them either.

The British didn't want to upset either group – they hate to create a scene – and so they managed, with a few nods, several winks and a couple of taps to the side of the nose, to give both sides the impression that they might be in the running for their own independent state. For example, they constantly changed the rules for Jewish immigration, sometimes, in response to Jewish pressure, opening Palestine's door wide, and at other times, in response to Arab pressure, slamming it shut. Matters weren't helped by the British refusal to take refugees into their own country.

As the Second World War approached, hostility between the Jews and the Arabs increased, and there were outbreaks of violence. The British were feeling stretched, and were keen to come to an arrangement between the two sides. They suggested creating two separate states – the Arabs refused the plan. They suggested creating a Jewish homeland in an Arab state – both sides rejected the idea. Eventually, after the Second World War, they threw their hands up in despair, flounced home for a cup of tea, and handed the problem over to the newly-formed United Nations.

I suppose that the UN was the fairest route for a resolution of the problem, but it was only young, and it didn't have the power to enforce its decision. It suggested that there be two separate states, one Jewish and one Arab. Jerusalem was to remain under international control. In 1947, the UN General Assembly accepted this suggestion. Britain and all Muslim countries voted against it.

As soon as the UN voted in favour of this arrangement, unofficial war broke out between the Jews and the Palestinian Arabs, as each side tried to expand its share of land. The Jews came off best during the fighting, mostly because their opponents were poorly-equipped and fragmented. In addition, the other Arab countries were not that bothered about helping their Arab brothers. By May in 1948, the Jews were in control of the area.

At this point, the other Arab countries made it clear that they would not accept an independent Jewish state. On the 14th May, the Jews went ahead and declared independence anyway. They did not define the borders of the new state of Israel at this point. Both sides were aware that borders would be decided by the coming war.

As soon as the Jews had declared their independence, Egypt, Transjordan, Syria, Lebanon and Iraq invaded. I would have thought that Israel didn't stand a chance against this group of nations, but the newly-formed Israeli Defence Force was actually stronger than the combined forces of its enemies. At the start of the war, 25,000 Arab troops lined up against 36,000 Israeli troops. Both sides increased their armies during the course of the fighting, but the Israelis always had a numerical advantage. Initially, Israel was less well-equipped, but this did not remain the case.

Most importantly, the Israelis were a single, well-organised unit, whereas the various Arab forces were not well coordinated, with each of the Arab countries having different aims. For example, Jordan and Israel have often been described as 'the best of enemies' both at the outbreak of the fighting in this conflict, and in later ones. Prior to the war, there existed a secret agreement between the two, in which they agreed to carve up British Palestine between them. Due to pressure from its Arab allies, Jordan could not be openly seen to honour this agreement. However, once the Jordanian troops had secured the land on the West Bank of the Jordan River (up to and including Eastern Jerusalem), they made no effort to take any of the lands that the UN had allocated to the Jews. The Jordan battle-plan pretty much stuck to the initial secret agreement.

Initially, the Israeli forces focused on securing their borders according to the UN, but, as they gained the upper hand in the fighting, they began to push on, and take some of the territory allocated to the Palestinian Arabs. The Israeli leader, David Ben-Gurion was all for continuing Israeli expansion, especially against Egypt, but the international community persuaded him otherwise, and Israel signed armistice agreements with each of the invading countries.

As a result of these agreements, Israel controlled all the land that the UN had allocated it (around 55% of British Palestine). In addition, it controlled a significant portion of the land allocated to the Palestinian Arabs – so that overall it controlled 79% of British Palestine. The remainder of British Palestine was shared between Egypt and Jordan. Egypt took the Gaza strip, which lay next to its border, and Jordan kept control of the West Bank and Israel and Jordan divided Jerusalem between themselves. There was a demilitarised zone on the Syrian border. Above all, there was no new state for the Palestinian Arabs.

And, that was the initial state of affairs. Israel's borders were defined by a UN plan that everybody ignored, and then by full-scale war. Tellingly, for a variety of complicated reasons, none of the armistice agreements ever turned into peace treaties, and so all the Arab countries technically remained at war with Israel. On top of that, they all refused to recognise Israel's right to exist. It didn't take long before war broke out again.

WHAT WAS THE SIX DAY WAR ALL ABOUT?

'The dowry pleases you but the bride does not.'
Levi Eshkol, Prime Minister of Israel from 1963-1969

'Our goal is clear – to wipe Israel off the map.'
President Aref of Iraq, May 31st 1967

I never believed that the Six Day War could have been all that serious. Six days just doesn't seem a period in which it is possible to achieve much. It is barely more than a working week – and I know how little I achieve during one of those. However, my initial assumption was wrong. It turns out that the Israeli Army is much more efficient in its use of time than I am. The Six Day War – which lasted from June 5th until June 11th 1967 – was a massive influence on the present situation in the Middle East.

According to one historian of the Arab–Israeli conflict, the Six Day War was the only one of the several conflicts between Israel and its neighbours that nobody wanted. It was the result of a chain reaction that got out of control. Everybody was feeling a bit tetchy. The Israelis were annoyed with the Syrians for allowing their country to be used as a base for attacks on Israel by Palestinian guerrillas led by Yasser Arafat. There was an incident in which an Israeli tractor was fired upon. It doesn't sound like much but it led to a dog fight between jets from the two countries over Syrian land. The Israelis made noises about a possible attack on Syria although they were probably not serious.

The Russians, for whom Syria was an important Cold War ally in the region, took them seriously though, and sent a message to Egypt claiming that the Israelis were massing on the Syrian border in preparation for invasion. The message was a lie, and there is confusion about who was responsible for it. The Egyptians probably knew this. But their leadership of the Arab states would have been called into question, if they had been seen to stand idle in the face of such a threat. So the Egyptian President, Gamal Abdel Nasser, mobilised his army, sending troops into the Sinai and requesting that a UN force on the Israeli border leave.

The Israeli government didn't know what to do. They had initially been fairly sure that Nasser had no real intention of going to war but was bluffing to save face but, as time went on, the feeling of real danger increased. The Israeli people began to panic. Military leaders called more and more forcibly for war. Yitzhak Rabin, the Chief of Staff for the Israeli Defence Force at the time, had a nervous breakdown. On the morning of June 5th 1967, Israel let loose its fighter jets, destroying the Egyptian and Jordanian air forces, and rendering the Iraqi and Syrian planes useless by bombing their airstrips.

As a result of their success in the air, Israeli troops were able to move forwards into Egypt with little difficulty. It seems that they were not quite prepared for such an easy victory. So quickly had they overpowered their enemies, their leaders were not entirely sure what they should do next. Initially, it seems, they only wanted to advance a little way into the Sinai, sign a ceasefire, and force the Egyptians to remove their troops from the area. But as they came to realise what a strong position they were in, the Israeli leaders ordered the troops onwards, until they had eventually taken the whole Sinai peninsula and were standing on the banks of the Suez canal.

It was the same on the other fronts. To begin with, the Israelis had shown little desire to move into Jordanian territory on the West Bank of the River Jordan, particularly because, although they were often on opposite sides in war, it was generally felt that Jordan was as close to an ally as was possible. But the Jordanians attacked a little too aggressively and the Israelis were forced to counter. Without air cover the Jordanians were quickly defeated and the Israelis overwhelmed the West Bank.

By this time, the Israeli command was feeling considerably more aggressive, deciding that they wanted to capture the Golan Heights in Syria as well. Although the UN called a ceasefire before it could do so, the Israelis chose to ignore it. It is even suggested that the Israelis attacked a US intelligence ship, the USS Liberty, killing thirty-four of its crew, in order to prevent their US allies from hearing about their actions. The Israelis have always claimed the attack was an accident. They made an apology which the US accepted.

On June 11th, Israel signed a ceasefire declaration with Syria, to join the ceasefires that they had already signed with Egypt and Jordan. As a result of six days of battle, they had taken control of the Sinai, the Gaza Strip, the West Bank and the Golan Heights, more than doubling the amount of land under Israeli control.

Initially, the Israelis made some noises about returning most of this land in exchange for peace treaties, but this was soon replaced by a desire to maintain their new position of strength in the region.

East Jerusalem was quickly made part of the state of Israel, fulfilling the Israeli dream of having a unified Jerusalem as their capital, but the rest of the land simply remained under military control which is why journalists and politicians commonly refer to them as the Occupied Territories. Israel returned the Sinai peninsula to Egypt (as part of a peace treaty signed in 1979), but the status of the remaining territories remains a matter of contention today.

In addition to the new land, the Israelis were now responsible for over a million Arabic people. The Palestinian Arabs, who felt ignored by the Arab countries and the international community as a whole, began to take matters more and more into their own hands. The coming years would see a rise in terrorist attacks on Israeli soil, and more and more strident demands from the Palestinian Arabs for a country of their own.

WHY CAN'T THEY ALL JUST GET ALONG?

'We were not prepared to relinquish three things: the security of Israel, those things that are holy to Israel, and the unity of our People. If we will be faced with the alternative between compromising one of these and a confrontation, the choice is clear to every Israeli.'
Israeli PM Ehud Barak after the Camp David peace talks, 2000

'It is clear and obvious [the Israelis] are trying to escape from implementing accurately and honestly what had been signed between both of us. I am not asking for the moon.'
Yasser Arafat

'Why can't they all just get along?' That was my initial reaction to the whole Middle Eastern situation. Why can't they just sit down and thrash out the issues, make a few compromises, shake hands and live happily ever after?

Then again, when you consider that people are capable of coming to blows over the correct line of a boundary fence, it is hardly surprising that the complicated tangle of issues that make up the Israel-Palestine conflict has, so far, proved impossible to unravel.

At least disagreements over boundary fences can be solved by appealing to concrete rules of ownership. But, in the Israel-Palestine conflict, this is exactly the problem. Who owns what land? There is no definitive answer to this question. It is the Jewish homeland but they were forced to leave by the Romans over two millennia ago. It is the Palestinian Arab homeland too. In the 40s, the UN suggested that both groups have their own country but the Israelis went on to establish their own borders after the First Arab–Israeli War. They expanded these borders in the Six Day War. Which facts do you choose to take as most significant?

It is not as if the various Middle Eastern players haven't been trying to settle these issues. Since the First Gulf War in 1990-1, for example, there have been a series of efforts by the Israelis and Palestinians to come to an agreement about the nature of a Palestinian state.

In 2000, Bill Clinton was coming to the end of his presidency. He invited Yasser Arafat, the leader of the Palestinian Liberation Organisation (PLO) and Ehud Barak, the Israeli prime minister, to come to Camp David (the US president's mountain retreat). He wanted them to try and settle their differences once and for all, and to come to a 'final status settlement', as the politicians like to call it. Sadly, the two sides, despite coming closer to agreement than ever before, could not manage it. But why? Why can't they all just get along? What are the problems that stand in the way?

There are all sorts of thorny issues involved. First of all, there is the issue of territory. Any Palestinian state would be created from the lion's share of what is called the West Bank. This was not allocated to Israel in the original UN plan for separate Arab and Jewish states put forward in 1947, nor did it lie within the original borders of Israel after the First Arab–Israeli War, which finished in 1949. In fact, at this point, it had been annexed by Jordan. It was only after the Six Day War of 1967, that it was taken over by the Israelis who never formally included it in the state of Israel, but governed it as an 'occupied territory' from then on.

It was very difficult to come to an agreement on how much territory was to be put aside for a Palestinian state, because of the very different ways in which the two sides viewed the issue. From a Palestinian perspective, they had already lost the majority of 'old'

Palestine to Israel in the First Arab-Israeli War. It seemed very unfair that Israel should do anything less than hand back control of the entire West Bank. From an Israeli point of view, they had gained control of the West Bank as the result of a legitimate war against Jordanian aggression. The Palestinians had never had their own state. They certainly didn't have the right to demand the return of the whole of the West Bank, especially if this would cause security issues for the state of Israel.

The situation was further complicated by the existence of Jewish settlements in the West Bank. The Israeli government wanted to draw the borders of the Palestinian state so that the majority of these remained in Israeli territory.

At the start of negotiations, Barak offered the Palestinians 66% of the West Bank, with a further 14% to be handed over in the near future. In his initial offer, this land would have been split into three 'islands' by corridors of Israeli territory that ran down to the River Jordan. 90% of the new Israeli settlements would have remained in Israel. The Palestinians felt that this proposition was totally unsatisfactory and rejected it out of hand.

A second problem was the status of Jerusalem. Once again, the Israelis had only controlled West Jerusalem since the end of the First Arab-Israeli War. They had taken East Jerusalem from Jordan in the Six Day War. Unlike the West Bank, it had been formally annexed and was now part of Israel. For the Israelis a unified Jerusalem containing the most sacred Jewish sites, was a dream come true. They would not consider having anything other than some form of unified Jerusalem as their capital. Yet Jerusalem contained some of the most sacred Muslim sites as well. The Palestinians were adamant that they must have some share of it.

In the event, Barak initially suggested that Israel have Jerusalem as its capital, whilst the Palestinians could have al-Quds, a collection of villages on the outskirts of Jerusalem, unconnected to the Old City. The Palestinians, however, wanted control over East

Jerusalem, and the Old City. In particular, they wanted some kind of ownership of the Temple Mount, which is of great importance to both Jews and Muslims alike.

The third major issue that divided the two sides was the question of refugees. During the First Arab-Israeli War, thousands of Palestinians had left their homes; some of them voluntarily, some of them against their will. They had been prevented from returning by the Israeli state. Arafat demanded that all these refugees, a population of around four million, be given the chance to return to their homes, or be compensated by the Israeli state. Against this suggestion, the Israelis argued that they were not responsible for the Palestinian refugees. They were prepared to allow a limited number of them to return, but the remainder should settle elsewhere. They should be paid compensation from an international fund to which the Israelis were happy to contribute.

Whilst these particular issues were hard enough to deal with, there were further general problems that made life even more difficult. For starters, both Arafat and Barak were limited in their ability to compromise by extremist groups. Barak could not afford to be seen to give away too much territory or to divide Jerusalem, for fear of losing control of the Israeli government to more conservative politicians.

More than that, extremist groups considered such actions to be a betrayal. Five years earlier, Prime Minister Yitzhak Rabin had been assassinated for just such a perceived betrayal. So fearful was Barak of leaving evidence for his right-wing opponents that he refused to write down any of his negotiating positions at Camp David on paper, or to meet with Arafat face-to-face. All his suggestions were presented verbally to the Americans, who then presented them to the Palestinians.

As it turned out, public opinion already felt Barak had gone too far with his compromises. He quickly lost his position after the Camp David meetings, and was replaced by the right-wing politician, Ariel Sharon.

On the Palestinian side, Arafat could not be seen to give too much ground either. Criticism was growing about the ineffectiveness of his leadership. He had promised to bring the whole West Bank under Palestinian rule, and to have Jerusalem as the capital of a new Palestinian state. If he failed in these promises, the more extreme Palestinian movements were likely to take control.

On top of that, there remained the deep suspicion that each side had for one another: the result of years of violence and bloodshed. Arafat might have been the chairman of the Palestinian Liberation Organisation, but the Fatah movement, of which he was the leader, had started off as a terrorist organisation, planning attacks on Israel from its position of exile in various other countries. As a result, the Israelis viewed Arafat with deep suspicion.

There was no love lost in the opposite direction either. Although Barak had a reputation as a moderate leader, he had not given this impression to the Palestinians as the Israeli prime minister. Probably in order to keep the right-wing factions of the government on side, he had encouraged the enlargement of Israeli settlements in the West Bank, and failed to honour some prior agreements. It was not clear to the Palestinians that he could be trusted.

Ultimately, despite compromises on both sides, the negotiations at Camp David failed. It is difficult to know exactly what was offered, due to Barak's refusal to commit on paper, but it is generally agreed that both sides went about as far as they could – although, at the time, Arafat was blamed for the failure of the talks.

At Camp David, or at subsequent meetings in the following months, Israel considered handing over 95% of the West Bank to the Palestinians, the two sides considered splitting East Jerusalem between them and arranging some kind of joint authority for Jerusalem, and the Palestinians considered mechanisms for preventing any significant return of refugees to Israel.

But whilst these compromises were being discussed, the tension between the two countries was bubbling to the surface again. At the end of 2000, Ariel Sharon visited the Temple Mount. Many see the visit as a political gambit. He wanted to demonstrate Israeli authority over the holy site, and undermine the ongoing negotiations. As a result of his visit, riots broke out. In the face of this violence, the Israelis turned to Sharon and his promises of security. In early 2001, he became prime minister. The violence continued. It was the start of the Second Intifada – several years of bloody conflict between the Israeli army and the Palestinian militia. The issues that caused the failure of the Camp David discussion remain to this day.

DOES THE PLO STILL EXIST?

'I come bearing an olive branch in one hand, and the freedom
fighter's gun in the other. Do not let the olive branch fall from
my hand...'
Yasser Arafat in an address to the UN, November 1974

It is strange how world news can allow an organisation to slip
into obscurity. For years, the PLO was one of the leading players
in the Israel-Palestine conflict, representing the Palestinian point
of view at summits and conferences. Yet, it occurred to me the
other day that I couldn't remember the last time I had heard it
mentioned. Had it been disbanded or did it still have a role to
pay? I had absolutely no idea.

The PLO was initially set up by the Arab League, a group of
Arab nations, in 1964. The Egyptian leader, Gamal Abdel Nasser
intended to use it as a control on the various Palestinian guerrilla
groups that had set up shop in the countries surrounding Israel.
Wary of a repeat of the 1948 Arab-Israeli war, which had allowed
Israel to establish itself in the region, he did not want these groups
to provoke another conflict. For their part, the guerrilla groups
had nothing to do with the new organisation.

The PLO contained representatives from various Palestinian
groups, who formed the Palestinian National Council. It had a
leadership, called the PLO Executive Committee, in whose hands
lay most of its power. It had an army – the Palestinian Liberation
Army. And it had a charter, which called for total liberation –
in part because of the prevailing influence at the time of Pan-

Arabism, Nasirism, and the attraction of Arab unity. (It wasn't until 1974 – the year of Yasser Arafat's address to the UN – that the PLO began to speak of a Palestinian state.) The PLO did not recognise the existence of Israel.

As it turned out, Nasser was unable to avoid another fight with Israel. In the 1967 Six Days War, Egypt and its allies were heavily defeated, and Israel occupied the West Bank, the Gaza Strip, the Golan Heights and the whole of the Sinai up to the Suez Canal. From this time on, the Arab countries lost their control over the PLO, and it quickly came to be dominated by the Palestinian guerrilla groups that it had set out to control.

The largest of these was Fatah, which had been set up by Yasser Arafat and his colleagues at the end of the 1950s, with the sole aim of defeating Israel and replacing it with a Palestinian state. 'Fatah' is a reverse acronym of the group's full name – the Palestinian National Liberation Movement – but also means 'conquest' in Arabic. Arafat couldn't use the straightforward acronym, because its Arabic translation was 'sudden death', and that didn't quite capture the image that he wanted to portray.

After the Six Day War, Fatah attracted thousands of recruits to continue the struggle against Israel, and Arafat proved a dab hand at finding financial backing for his mission. He established himself as the leading Palestinian figure, and he was elected as president of the PLO in 1969, a position which he retained until his death in 2004. Fatah dominated the leadership of the organisation throughout this time.

After Arafat and Fatah assumed control of it, the PLO became the biggest thorn in Israel's side. It was an umbrella group for a variety of organizations, many of which launched small-scale attacks, carried out hijackings, and generally made life difficult. Israel refused to recognise it as the legitimate voice of the Palestinian people. In fact, the Israelis were very keen to see it destroyed.

Under Arafat, the PLO initially set up shop in Jordan, but

was driven out by the Jordanians, who became fed up with its lawlessness. So, the PLO moved the centre of its operations to Lebanon. However, in the early 1980s, Israel invaded the country in order to drive them out once more. Arafat escaped again, this time to establish the PLO HQ in Tunisia.

It took a long time, but the PLO eventually established itself on the world stage as the representative of the Palestinian people. In 1974 the Arab states recognised it as the legitimate voice of the Palestinians, and shortly afterwards it was allowed observer status at the UN. The USA took longer to come on board, insisting that it give up terrorism and recognise Israel, but by the end of the 1980s it was generally willing to deal with PLO representatives. During this period, the PLO relied less and less on the use of violence, although attacks were still carried out in its name.

In 1993 there was a further significant development, in the shape of the Oslo Accords: it was the first time that the Israelis and Palestinians had sat down opposite one another and tried to come up with a solution to their problems. Yasser Arafat met with the Israeli Prime Minister, Yitzhak Rabin, agreeing to recognise the existence of the state of Israel, to renounce terrorism, and to negotiate towards the creation of a separate Israel and Palestine. In response to this Rabin agreed to recognise the PLO as the representative of the Palestinians.

As a result of this agreement and the negotiations that followed, Israel promised to withdraw from part of the Gaza Strip and the West Bank, and to hand over control of these areas to a new Palestinian Authority.

Sadly, the peace process started by the Oslo Accords faltered, and then failed. The Palestinians, frustrated at what they felt to be the bad faith of the Israelis, rose against them again in 2000 in the Second Intifada. Since then, there has been precious little progress towards a final two-state solution, and plenty of violence.

Unsurprisingly, the new Palestinian Authority was dominated by Arafat and his Fatah movement. Arafat was elected its president of in early 1996. After his death, he was succeeded by his Fatah colleague, Mahmoud Abbas. Fatah continued in government until they lost the parliamentary elections to Hamas in 2006.

However, the PLO continues to be the official representative of Palestinians worldwide (and most Palestinians live overseas). The PLO is still Israel's official negotiations partner, and if there could ever be agreement on what happens to Palestinian refugees, it would have to be the PLO that makes the final decision and implements this.

This does not appear to be common knowledge. In recent discussions, several experts assured me that the PLO still exists, but that it no longer plays an important role in ongoing events. In fact, they were at a loss to say what the true current role of the PLO actually is. It is not often, in my telephone conversations with academics, that I ask a question to which they don't know the answer. Thankfully there was one that put me straight.

HOW DID HAMAS WIN AN ELECTION?

'I don't trust the term "moderate". We are already moderate.
But if people believe we will be moderate in the Western style,
or a pro-Israeli style – that's not moderate. That's corruption.'
Mahmud al-Zahar, Hamas's deputy leader, 5th September 2005

Hamas's victory in the 2006 Palestinian elections for the Palestinian parliament came as a big surprise to the international community. I am a member of the international community – and I was no exception. As far as I knew, Hamas was a terrorist organisation with a liking for suicide bomb attacks. I wasn't even aware that it was a serious political contender with the ability to win the elections.

Hamas came into existence in 1987 and its name is an acronym for the full name of the movement which is the Islamic Resistance Movement. It also happens to be the Arabic word for 'zeal'. It was founded by Sheikh Ahmed Yassin as a branch of the Muslim Brotherhood, an international Muslim organisation with branches in many countries.

At the time of its founding the Palestinians in the Occupied Territories were fed up with their lot. There appeared to be no chance of achieving any kind of self-rule and their daily existence was made difficult by the Israelis. In recent years, the Israeli government had launched an 'Iron Fist' policy, aimed at crushing all resistance to their rule. Palestinians were detained without trial and were regularly beaten. The legal system gave them no protection.

The Muslim Brotherhood joined the multitude of groups that had set up shop to provide services to the Palestinians, and to create some sense of community for them. These groups were involved in public works: anything from building hospitals to setting up soup kitchens. However, at the end of 1987, the Palestinians rose up against the Israelis in the uprising known as the Intifada. The members of Hamas joined in the fighting with their compatriots.

In 1988 Hamas produced its charter, in which it stated that its ultimate purpose was to dismantle the country of Israel – or the 'Zionist entity' as Hamas preferred to call it – and replace it with a Muslim state. (The Hamas military wing is known as the Izz al-Din al-Qassam brigades, after a resistance hero from the Mandate era.)

From this point onwards, Hamas has simultaneously provided social services to the Palestinian people and continued its attacks on Israel. It has always opposed the various peace negotiations that have taken place since the end of the Intifada on the grounds that they accept the existence of Israel. It opposes the PLO for taking part in these negotiations, and until recently it opposed the Palestinian Authority, since it is the result of these negotiations.

To the international community, Hamas has become famous for its use of suicide bombers. Its struggle with Israel has been a very dirty war, with both sides resorting to repellent tactics. Hamas was responsible for the infamous 'Passover' bombing in March 2002. A member of the Hamas military wing walked into a crowded hotel dining-room and detonated a bomb, which killed thirty people and injured 140 more.

Israel replied to Hamas's attacks by assassinating its leaders. In March 2004, Israeli helicopters shot down Sheikh Yassin as he was leaving a Gaza mosque. Yassin had been wheelchair-bound since a playground accident in his youth.

Hamas's social and community services and its unrelenting stance on Israel both played a part in its success in the elections in

2006. In both areas, it was able to present itself to the Palestinian people as an improvement on Fatah, the organisation founded by Yasser Arafat, and the ruling group in the PLO and the Palestinian Authority up until this point. Many were also attracted by Hamas's reputation for honesty in contrast to the crippled Palestinian Authority and Fatah's reputation for corruption.

Arafat and Fatah had made compromises with Israel in a gamble that this would lead to a Palestinian state but it seemed as if the gamble had failed. Daily life in the Occupied Territories was no better. The Israelis continued to expand their settlements in the West Bank and were building a massive security fence that contained West Bank territory within it.

As a result, Many Palestinians were attracted to Hamas's uncompromising attitude towards Israel, even if they did not necessarily support its long-term goal of a single Muslim state, or some of its methods.

I had assumed that most Palestinians would not be supportive of suicide bombings. In actual fact, several people I spoke with on the subject said that this was not necessarily the case. They said that, whilst the majority of Palestinians would not support suicide bombings outright, they would put forward some defence for their use. In the circumstances, Palestinians see that they have very little choice – suicide bombings are the only way in which to make their voices heard. Nor do the Israeli forces show much consideration for civilian lives in their operations.

However, in the 2006 elections attitudes towards Israel were not the most important factor in deciding their outcome. The Palestinians were fed up with Fatah's incompetence in running the day-to-day business of life in the Occupied Territories. They had had enough of the corruption in Fatah ranks. Arafat had made a show of living frugally, but his relations and cronies did not follow his example. Arafat's wife lived in Paris, subsidised by a hundred thousand dollars a month in funds from the Palestinian Authority.

In comparison, Hamas had a reputation for being corruption-free, and they had been running effective services in the West Bank and Gaza for two decades. For many Palestinians, a vote for Hamas was simply a vote for an improvement in the wretched conditions in which they lived.

Once Hamas was in control of the Palestinian parliament, the international community were at a bit of a loss over what to do about it. Immediately after the elections, the USA and the EU cut off funding to the Palestinian Authority. Israel refused to talk to Hamas unless it renounced violence and recognised its right to exist. Hamas, despite the claims in its charter, made it clear unofficially that it was willing to negotiate but it refused to take any official steps unless the Israelis offer them something in return. The peace process was at a dead end.

WHY ARE THE PALESTINIANS FIGHTING ONE ANOTHER?

'What is happening now is not only the collapse of the
Palestinian national unity government but actually the collapse
of the whole Palestinian Authority.'
Mustafa Barghouti, Palestinian Information Minister

Hamas won the Palestinian elections at the start of 2006. They refused to recognise the existence of Israel, or previous peace deals with the Israelis, or to give up terrorism. As a result, the world refused to deal with them. In particular, the USA and the EU cut off all financial aid.

After a year of wrangling and indecision, a new government was formed, the so-called national unity government. The new cabinet contained representatives from Hamas, as well as from their main rival Fatah, and several independents. The original Hamas prime minister, Ismail Haniyeh, continued his post, but the various ministries were shared amongst the different groups.

The new government didn't fare much better than the old. The international community, especially the US, continued to turn its back on it. Financial aid continued to be withheld. At the start of June, the new government collapsed as violence escalated in both the Gaza Strip and the West Bank. Hamas took control of Gaza, whilst the Palestinian president, Mahmoud Abbas, a member of Fatah, dissolved the government and declared a state of national emergency.

Abbas appointed a new prime minister, Salam Fayyad, an

independent politician, to put together an emergency government. Hamas refused to recognise this new government. They retained control over the Gaza Strip, whilst Abbas and the new government kept control over the West Bank. Fighting continued.

Throughout this period, the papers reported fighting between Hamas and Fatah. It was always the kind of story that appeared briefly every week or so, and then faded away – just enough to give the impression that the Occupied Territories were a mess, without really helping to understand why this might be the case. Even Hamas' takeover of Gaza, during which hundreds of people died, only made the front pages for a couple of days.

There was a feeling that it was just a slightly more violent continuation of what had gone before. It was nothing new. It was a background noise – a default state – for the region.

I remember a comment by a friend of mine: 'The Palestinians aren't doing much of a job at showing they can run their own country.'

My friend went on to elaborate. In the summer of 2006, the Israelis had withdrawn from the Gaza Strip. By doing so, they had, for the first time, given total control over part of the Occupied Territories to the Palestinians. Instead of taking this as an opportunity, the Palestinians had promptly gone about fighting with one another. How could they expect the world to take them seriously?

Well, in answer to this questions, conditions in Gaza and the West Bank are not normal. There is huge frustration at the peace process. For many Palestinians, life has got worse since its start in the form of the Oslo Accords in 1993. The Palestinian economy has been ruined by decades of occupation. There is massive unemployment – around 75% of the youth in Gaza don't have jobs. Violence has increased. Israeli settlements have continued to grow in the West Bank. And there appears to be no possibility of a genuine Palestinian state any time soon. In conditions like these, it is unlikely that rivals are going to be able to sit down and calmly discuss their differences.

Against this background, an increasingly tense power struggle between the two rival organisations of Fatah and Hamas has developed. Since it was formed by Yasser Arafat and his allies in the late 1950s, Fatah has been the leading player in the Palestinian movement. It controlled the PLO, which was the recognised voice of the Palestinian people at the Oslo Accords, and, until 2006, it controlled the Palestinian Authority, which grew out of the Accords. It has been the establishment voice of the Palestinians for a couple of decades. Hamas, formed in the late 1980s, has challenged Fatah's authority. It has grown in support, popularity and influence, until finally coming to power in the 2006 parliamentary elections.

Although both groups want an independent Palestine for the Palestinian people, there are massive differences between them. Fatah is committed to following in the footsteps of the Oslo Accords in the search for a two-state solution. It has negotiated towards this with the West and Israel in the past, and continues to do so. It wants a secular state. Many of its leaders spent a number of years in exile with the PLO. It is the stronger group in the West Bank.

In contrast, Hamas refuses to accept the Oslo Accords which it regards as a sell-out to the Israelis and it is vigorously anti-Israel. It wants a Muslim state for the Palestinians. Its leadership is local. It is the stronger group in the Gaza Strip and it is especially popular with the poorer sections of Palestinian society.

A Hamas follower would be likely to say that the Fatah leaders are the corrupt puppets of the Western world with little understanding of the local people. In fact, that is exactly what the Hamas fighters did say over the loudspeakers in Gaza as they took control. A Fatah follower would say that Hamas is a violent extremist group with no desire for peace. Both views are an exaggeration of the truth.

Because of these differences and because of the growing rivalry between the two movements, there has been no love lost between them for the last couple of decades. Given the frustrations of the Palestinian people, the fact that these differences have not been settled peacefully is hardly surprising. It hasn't helped that the Occupied Territories are awash with weapons, or that both groups have their own militias to help protect them.

In the 1990s, Mohammed Dahlan, the Fatah security chief of the Palestinian Authority, led an aggressive campaign against Hamas in an attempt to destroy it. He was supported in this by Israel and the West. He became a hate-figure for Hamas and its followers. In some respects, the recent Hamas campaign in Gaza can be seen as revenge for these actions. After the 1990s, Dahlan remained a key figure in the Fatah presence in Gaza. One of the strongest images from the recent fighting was of two Hamas militants kicking his door down, and taking possession of his residence. Fortunately for Dahlan, he was not in.

Even though Fatah and Hamas have carried out sporadic attacks on one another for some time, things got much worse after the Hamas victory in the 2006 elections, since when the Palestinians have teetered on the edge of civil war. The events of June may well have pushed them over the edge. Commentators say that they have been surprised by the intensity of the violence over the last couple of years. They are also keen to stress that it is not normal. Up until 2006, ordinary Palestinians did not fight with one another.

So what has changed since 2006? First of all, the international response to Hamas's election has made the already difficult conditions in the Occupied Territories even worse. The USA and the EU refused to provide essential financial aid – even when the government of national unity was formed at the start of 2007. Israel also refused to hand over hundreds of millions of dollars in tax revenue. Without all this money, the Palestinian government was unable to pay salaries. Unsurprisingly, feelings ran high amongst the people.

In addition, it seems likely that Hamas became more and more frustrated with the international community's refusal to deal with it. The organisation gave out mixed messages about its intentions, partly because it has several competing leaders, but the general consensus was that it was prepared to negotiate. It was a pragmatic organisation. It knew that its charter goal of displacing Israel with a single Palestinian state was not realistic but it was not prepared to give up this goal until Israel showed the willingness to offer something reasonable in its place.

From Hamas's point of view, it was the democratically elected government. Yet, at the start of 2007, it was given little choice but to join forces with Fatah and other independents in the government of national unity. In particular, it was frustrated by Fatah's continuing control over most of the security forces.

It is not clear what is going to happen now. To all intents and purposes, the Occupied Territories have now split into two, with Abbas and Fatah controlling the West Bank, and Hamas controlling Gaza. It seems likely that conditions will deteriorate in Gaza, since Israel are unlikely to deal with Hamas in arranging for deliveries of fuel and power supplies.

A confidential UN report was recently leaked in which the outgoing Middle East envoy summed up his impressions of the last couple of years. In his view, nobody came out favourably. The Palestinians have a poor record of controlling violence. The Israelis have made unrealistic demands on the new Hamas government. The international community's refusal to recognise Hamas, and its withdrawal of financial support has made everything much worse.

So, it seems, that whilst Hamas and Fatah have plenty of responsibility for what has happened, they are not the only ones. The recent events in the Occupied Territories did not happen in a vacuum – but have been influenced by the actions of various different governments around the world.

FURTHER READING

Gelvin, James L. *The Israel-Palestine Conflict: 100 Years of War*, Cambridge: Cambridge University Press (2005).

Hirst, David, *The Gun and the Olive Branch*, London: Faber and Faber (2003).

Pappe, Ilan, *A History of Modern Palestine: One land, Two Peoples*, Cambridge: Cambridge University Press (2006).

Shlaim, Avi, *The Iron Wall: Israel and the Arab World*, London: Penguin (2000).

Tessler, Mark, *A History of the Israeli-Palestinian Conflict*, Indiana: Indiana University Press (1994).

DARFUR:
AGGRIEVED
ACRONYMS

WHO LIVES IN DARFUR?

'The problem with the public discussion of Darfur and Sudan is
not simply that we know so little; it is also the representation of
what we do know.'
Mahmood Mamdani. Pambazuka News, October 7th 2004

There is a definite tendency amongst humans to boil things
down to two sides. Black and white with no shades in between.
Capitalism against communism. The battle of the sexes. Tom
versus Jerry. To name but a few examples. The Darfur conflict is
no exception to this rule. Along with many other disputes these
days, it is normally represented as a fight between Arabs and non-
Arabs. You can therefore be forgiven for thinking that there are
just two tribes in Darfur – or that, if there are more, that it is easy
to place them into one of these categories. But this is just not
true.

Depending on how you decide to classify an ethnic group,
there are between forty and ninety of them in the Darfur region.
Some of them have lived here for many centuries, amongst them
the Fur, the Masalit and the Zaghawa. Others have drifted in
from other regions of Africa over the years. In particular, nomadic
Arab tribes migrated to Darfur between the 14th and the 18th
centuries, where they travelled back and forth along traditional
routes, herding cattle or camels.

Ancestry and ethnicity remain important, but the various
groups have been coexisting for a pretty long time and they
haven't kept themselves to themselves. They have lived together in

settlements for centuries, during which there has been plenty of intermarriage. It is not often possible to distinguish between the various groups. There are dark-skinned 'Arabs' and pale-skinned 'Africans'.

More importantly, the various inhabitants of Darfur don't necessarily define themselves as being from any particular ethnic group. They may have connections to several of them. Or the distinctions between different groups may become so blurred over the centuries that they no longer have any meaning.

The common language in Darfur is Arabic. Alongside this, a Darfurian might well speak his own language and several other local ones. Some 'African' groups have lost their own languages over time, and now speak only Arabic. All Darfurians are Muslims of one kind or another – so it's hard to argue that any conflict between them is religious.

This is not to say that the history of the Darfur region has been a model of harmony. It is a difficult place to make a living. Much of it is incredibly dry. Water and fertile land are hard to come by. So, there have always been arguments and small-scale conflicts over resources in which different groups have come to blows. But, in general, these arguments have been settled by inter-tribal negotiations where both sides have felt that justice has been done.

Most importantly, the divisions that arose out of these disputes did not run along Arab versus non-Arab lines – that was not part of the equation. In thirteen major disagreements between groups over the period 1957-1990, the main issues were always access to land, pasture and grazing, as well as theft of livestock. Only four of these arguments were between an Arab group and a non-Arab group, and only one of these was accompanied by racial prejudice.

Just to prove how flexible ethnic divisions have been in the Darfur region, over its history it has been perfectly possible for individuals to move from one group to another. From the 17th century to the 19th century, most of the modern-day Darfur region was under the governance of a Fur-dominated sultanate. This is where the name 'Darfur' came from – it means 'land of the Fur'. In fact, the historical fear of Fur domination explains some of the splits in the current rebel movements, which are made up from several different groups.

The sultanate was a fairly loose structure. The various groups followed Islam and spoke Arabic, but were generally left to look after their own affairs, as long as they accepted the authority of the Fur leaders and paid tribute. However, during times of hardship, and the climate of Darfur ensures that there are plenty of these, it was not uncommon for members of other groups to become Fur, in order to share in the protection that this gave them.

More recently, there was a study of the make-up of a typical North Darfurian village. Its people referred to themselves as Fur-Zaghawa, and they all spoke Fur, Zaghawa and Arabic. There were plenty of other groups there as well with their various other languages. In this village, if a Fur farmer managed to purchase a few more animals and decided to migrate with them to find pasture, he might start referring to himself as 'Zaghawa', or even 'Arab'.

It is only really since the 1980s that the people of Darfur have been encouraged to think of themselves as either Arab or non-Arab, and to line up against each other in conflicts along these lines, despite the fact that this distinction ignores the mixed background of all Darfurians. The blame for this lies partly with the influence of an Arab supremacist philosophy that filtered into the area from Libya, and partly with the Sudanese government's support of groups that defined themselves as 'Arab'.

Dividing the groups into Arabs and non-Arabs might help to make the situation in Darfur more digestible for us but it hides the historical tensions between the various groups and distorts the true nature of the conflict.

WHO ARE THE JANJAWEED?

'The janjaweed are like a grotesque mixture of the Mafia and the
Klu Klux Klan.'
John Prendergast, International Crisis Group

In every news report we see on Darfur, the Janjaweed lurk as
the shadowy villains of the piece, accused of horrific war crimes
against innocent victims. Even their name is impressively sinister,
like some dark force out of Star Wars. But we are very rarely given
any background for them.

In actual fact, the Janjaweed form only a tiny minority of the
various Arab groups in Darfur, most of which have tried to remain
neutral in the current conflict. NGOs report that many Arab
groups find it insulting that the Janjaweed are described as 'Arab
militia' in international newspapers arguing that the Janjaweed
are in no way representative of Darfurian Arabs. In reality, the
situation is more confused – there are Arabs fighting with the
rebels, and there are non-Arabs fighting with the Janjaweed.

Darfur is a complicated place with umpteen different tribes,
some of them of Arab descent, some of them of African descent.
For centuries, they have rubbed along fairly happily. For example,
the Arab nomadic tribes used to act as herdsmen for the livestock
of African farmers.

However, for a variety of reasons, relationships between some
of the groups began to become frayed over the last few decades.
First of all, there were terrible droughts in the early 1980s. The
land of Darfur has always been split between farmland for its

(mostly African) farmers and pastureland available for the (mostly Arab) nomads. However, lack of rain put pressure on this system. Other tribes drifted into Darfur from more arid areas. The farmers became more possessive of their pastureland, putting fences in the way of the nomads.

For many nomads, their way of life became unsustainable. They tried to settle, but were forced to rely on poor land granted to them by farmers. They struggled to make ends meet by offering themselves as hired labour in the settlements and the farms. It was a difficult existence, and led to resentment over land.

Secondly, the balance of society was affected by influences from outside the area. In 1985, a military coup brought about a change of the Sudanese government. The new government quickly allied itself to Colonel Muammar al-Gadafi's Libya. In particular, it turned a blind eye to Gadafi's use of Darfur as a base to support the operations of Arab rebel groups in neighbouring Chad.

At this time, Gadafi had a vision of creating an 'Arab belt'. His first priority was Chad, which was governed by a Christian and 'African' leadership. Throughout the 1980s, Gadafi tried to bring down the Chad government, going as far as proclaiming the union of Chad and Libya in 1981. He was finally forced to change his tune in 1987 when Libyan troops were soundly beaten by Chadian government forces in the desert.

Gadafi's extravagant plans introduced unwelcome new factors to the delicate balance of life in Darfur. For a start, it brought in truckloads of weapons. In 1990, it was possible to buy a Kalashnikov rifle for 40 dollars. The influx of arms led to a rise in banditry, which the Sudanese government did not have the resources to deal with. It also undermined the traditional way of dealing with conflict. In the past, blood money had been paid to settle tribal feuds. But blood money was not a suitable way of dealing with the carnage caused by modern weapons. Conflicts became confused and far more deadly. It was often impossible to know who was responsible for the deaths of whom.

On top of the guns came the unwelcome notion of Arab supremacy. Gadafi's project contained within it the idea that Arabs were superior to the African tribes. In fact, there had always been an element of superiority in the Arabs' attitudes, but the 1980s saw these attitudes become more aggressive. In Darfur, leaflets began to appear printed by a group called the 'Arab Gathering'. These claimed that Arabs formed a majority in Darfur and urged the various Arab groups to unite in order to control the Darfurian administration. Then came organised attacks on non-Arabs. The same 'Arab Gathering' sent letters to the Sudanese government demanding more power for Darfurian Arabs, and hinting at possible violent consequences if these demands were not met.

As a result of the combination of pressure on land, tensions between different groups, and the increased number of weapons, fighting became more prolonged towards the end of the 1980s as various groups attacked one another. For the first time, these attacks began to split along Arab–African lines. Neither side was innocent of brutality.

It was at this time that the term '*janjaweed*' first came in to use to describe Arab militias, who carried out violent attacks on the African tribes, the most numerous of which were the Fur. The word had previously been applied to 'bandits', but also contained echoes within it of the words for rifle, devil and horse. Some of these men were recent immigrants from the fighting in Chad. Others were home grown groups.

Despite peace talks between various factions in 1989, relations did not improve. During the 1990s, the African groups began to feel that the Sudanese government was discriminating against them. They were fed up with the lack of investment in Darfur by the central government, with the government's bias towards local Arab groups and with its reluctance to protect them from attacks by Arab militias. In protest, a rebel movement began to grow.

The Sudanese government, whose army was already occupied in a war against tribes in the south of the country, looked for other means of fighting this new campaign. They recruited fighters from the poorest Arab groups, who had bones to pick with the non-Arab farming groups over land and access to water and who were the most influenced by ideas of Arab supremacy.

The result was the Janjaweed militias, who fought the government's war for it, torturing and raping their victims and burning their houses and crops. The sections of the government army that were present in Darfur made no effort to prevent these attacks and were viewed by many of the African farmers as no better than Janjaweed itself. The Janjaweed attacks continue to this day.

Still, repellent as the Janjaweed are, they are not the only group responsible for the current carnage. Elements of the rebel groups have adopted similar tactics. Whilst the main thrust of the fighting is between rebel groups on the one hand and the Janjaweed and government forces on the other, there is plenty of infighting on both sides and there are other armed groups who have simply taken advantage of the chaos to make a profit.

Of the fifty-one individuals that a UN report on the conflict recommended should be the subject of investigation by an international court, ten were from the central Sudanese government, seventeen were from the local government, fourteen were janjaweed commanders, three were from foreign armies, and seven were rebel commanders. It seems that the only people who are really innocent are the people who are caught in the crossfire.

WHO ARE THE SUDANESE REBELS?

'The Kalash(nikov) brings cash; without a Kalash you're trash.'
Modern Darfurian saying

The problem with an acronym is that it doesn't give you anything to hold on to. There is no hint of the connection between the assortment of letters that make it up and the object that it describes. As a result, I find that acronyms slide over my memory like raindrops on a windscreen, leaving absolutely no trace of their passage.

Another problem is that several organisations tend to share the same one. The JEM is both a Darfurian rebel movement and a Japanese car servicing company in North London.

The Darfur rebel movement is full of acronyms. There is the SLM/A, which used to be the DLF, and which must not be confused with the SPLM/A. Then, of course, there is the JEM, from which the NMRD split in 2004. But who are these people and what do they want?

Very roughly, there are two rebel groupings. The first of these is the Sudan Liberation Movement, and its military wing the Sudan Liberation Army, which emerged at the turn of the millennium. This group has a complicated leadership, but a couple of its major players are Minni Minnawi and Abdel Wahid. The SLM/A (to use its acronym) grew out of several separate resistance movements in Darfur.

During the 1980s, there was growing conflict amongst Darfurian groups over land, water, and pasture for nomadic herdsmen.

Government forces were either unable to do anything about it or had no desire to intervene. In defence, several of the tribes (most notably the Fur, the Masalit, and the Zaghawa) formed their own militias to protect themselves against these attacks. Most of the recruits to these forces were farmers, but some of them were teachers and doctors who had seen schools and clinics destroyed.

As time went on, frustration grew amongst the various tribes at the continued violence, and it began to take on an ethnic dimension with both Arabs and non-Arabs claiming that the other side wished to wipe them out. Darfurians also felt that the Sudanese government had no interest in developing their region. They saw no improvement in its infrastructure. Their children were denied a decent education, their women had to walk for hours each day in search of water and their men were given few opportunities in the administration of the region.

The Fur resistance began to reach out to the other tribes and form alliances, first with the Zaghawa and then with the Masalit. Initially, the other tribes were reluctant to get involved, but the growing violence of attacks by the Janjaweed militias from impoverished Arab tribes changed their minds.

For example, in 2001 the Janjaweed attacked the Zaghawa village of Abu Gamra killing 125 people. Amongst these were thirty-six people who were attending a meeting for the reopening of the village's primary schools, including their two head teachers. I don't know about you, but when I read about such events I find it almost impossible to believe that they can actually be true.

The Zaghawa and the Masalit fighters joined the Fur forces in their bases in the Jebel Marra massif in the centre of Darfur, from which they began to launch attacks on police stations and other government institutions. They targeted the government because they blamed the problems of Darfur on its refusal to invest in the area and because they suspected that it was supporting the Janjaweed militias. The SLM/A really announced itself in April 2003, when it attacked a military base in the town of al-Fashir, destroying aircraft and killing soldiers.

The various groups represented in the SLM/A are not natural allies. There has been rivalry between the tribes over the years. The Zaghawa, in particular, who, unlike the other two groups, are traditionally nomadic, had more often than not sided with the other nomadic Arab tribes in local disputes. Despite these differences, the group tried to maintain a united front, electing a representative of each tribe to its top leadership positions. It also has representatives from other tribes, including several commanders from Arab ones.

But as the movement has grown – support flocked to it after the al-Fashir incident – it has struggled to hold its various internal factions together and there have been outbreaks of fighting between them. Its leaders are not experienced in war or in negotiations and often send their orders from outside the country. This state of affairs has prompted diplomats at peace negotiations to say that the SLM/A is not one organisation, but several.

The second rebel grouping is called the Justice and Equality Movement (JEM). Its most prominent leader is Dr. Khalil Ibrahim, and it announced itself openly on the scene in August 2001. JEM was set up by Darfurian politicians and students in Khartoum in the 1990s. These people had initially been supportive of the Islamic Sudanese government which had come to power in 1989 but they became disillusioned when it showed no interest in developing Darfur or helping to solve its many problems.

In 2000, they anonymously published the 'Black Book'. This book gave statistics showing how much of the power in the country had been kept by a handful of tribes from the north of the country, who formed only about 5% of the country's population. Every president had come from their ranks, as had the vast majority of military and political leaders. The JEM leadership decided that the only way to change this state of affairs was to fight.

Although the JEM draws much of its support from a particular branch of the Zaghawa tribe, it has presented itself as a national organisation, and contains representatives from tribes all over the country. Its stated aim is to end the government's neglect of many of Sudan's outlying areas. However the JEM too has suffered from internal divisions

The SLM/A and JEM have very different backgrounds, but they have formed both military and political alliances during the course of the conflict because of their similar aims. Both organisations say that they are fighting against the government's policy of preference for Darfurian Arab groups. They both state that they want all Sudan's regions to have representation at government level, to have some level of autonomy over their own affairs and to have an equal share in the development of Sudan.

Initially, the rebel military campaign was very successful. It defeated government forces again and again in 2003, attacking quickly with Toyota land cruisers in small but effective raids. The Sudanese army was poorly-organised and not trained to deal with this type of warfare. But the situation changed as the government threw its support behind militias from the Arab tribes – the janjaweed.

In peace negotiations as well the two movements have struggled to build on their initial momentum, hampered by their internal divisions and the inexperience of their leaders. At the end of 2006, an MSF report suggested that there were as many as twelve separate factions between the rebel groupings, of which only three had signed up to peace negotiations in the Nigerian capital of Abuja.

There have been incidents of fighting between the factions and The Sudanese government has used these flaws to present them as an ineffective group with which to do business. A peace treaty was signed in Nigeria in May 2006, but several of the rebel factions did not support it, and the peace process has stalled.

The situation in Darfur is dire, and it is no longer possible to tell who is fighting whom. The government continues to battle (unsuccessfully for the most part) with the rebel groups who did not sign up to the Abuja treaty. The rebel groups, unable to decide on the best course of action, are fighting amongst themselves. And tribal clashes have once more broken out over the age-old problems of access to pasture and water – only now everyone has a gun.

WHAT IS THE SUDANESE
GOVERNMENT UP TO?

'When the problems with the rebels started in Darfur, we in the
government of Sudan had a number of options. We chose the
wrong one, the very worst one.'
Lt. Gen. Ibrahim Suleiman, quoted in
The New York Times Magazine, October 17th 2004

'The Sudanese government needs to bring war criminals to
justice, not recruit them into positions of responsibility.'
Peter Takirambudde, Human Rights Watch, Africa

The Sudanese government of Omar al-Bashir doesn't have a
particularly good reputation. Its leaders are famous for backing
Saddam Hussein's invasion of Kuwait and for allowing Osama bin
Laden to make Khartoum his second home. It has been in charge
of the country during the unpleasant war with rebels in the south
and during the crisis in Darfur.

Internally, though, the government's standing has not always
been so low. In 1985, the Sudanese president, Gaafar el-Nimeiry,
was overthrown in a military coup. He was replaced, in 1986, by
a coalition government of various Islamic parties, which, in its
turn, would be overthrown in another coup in 1989. From that
time on Omar al-Bashir has been in charge of the country. His
party, the National Congress Party, is still technically Islamist, but
self-interest is the real motivation behind its policies.

When the Islamists first came to power they had considerable support in many areas, including Darfur. It was felt that the Islamist leaders were honest and hard-working. They portrayed themselves as a unifying force who would overcome the tribal divisions that had caused trouble in previous governments. In the early 90s, the Sudanese government launched a massive social campaign, sending out idealistic Islamic teachers to villages and encouraging Islamic philanthropic organisations to set up hospitals and schools.

But as time went on, it became clear that this new government was no better than the ones that had gone before it. It continued to be dominated by a handful of tribes from the banks of the Nile in the northern part of the country. These tribes ruled the country for their own benefit and with little regard for the people in its other regions. In 2000, this disillusionment was summed up by the secret publication of the 'Black Book' by various leaders in the growing Darfur rebel movement.

The al-Bashir government was intent on controlling Sudan's regions. In Darfur, the top regional positions went to members of al-Bashir's party who were not necessarily from the Darfur region. Al-Bashir also began to build alliances with particular Darfurian groups. As a rule, the groups he supported classified themselves as 'Arab' – even though, after centuries of coexistence and intermarriage the distinction between 'Arab' and 'non-Arab' was by no means a clear one.

To give an idea of the kind of manoeuvring the government got up to, one thing it did was to split the Darfur region into three provinces. I wouldn't have thought that the redrawing of some boundaries could be a particularly hostile move – but the split was cleverly designed so that the Fur ethnic group, which was the largest of the many Darfurian groups, became a minority in all three of the new provinces. As a result, the Fur lost out on administrative power.

Other groups were just as unhappy about the state of affairs. The Masalit, another important Darfurian group, suspected that the position of their chief as one of the most influential leaders in the region was under threat from the government's changes to the administration. Their dissatisfaction grew until in the mid-90s it resulted in armed resistance in the Masalit Wars, which reportedly claimed 2000 lives, and displaced 100, 000 people.

At the root of all this discontent was the government's failure to invest in Darfur or to allow its people any real role in the country's affairs. In the first two years of humanitarian assistance as much money was pumped into the region as had been allocated to it by the government since independence. At the start of the conflict, there were eleven doctors in Darfur. Now, through all the various NGOs, there are hundreds.

The unrest in the area did not go away but spread elsewhere. By 2000, the government was facing opposition from a variety of different sources. Initially it tried to stamp out the rebellion but was largely unsuccessful. At the start of the conflict much of the army was occupied with the continued war against rebels in the south of the country, which had been in progress, on and off, for a couple of decades. On top of this, many of the rank and file in the army were from the Darfur region – and the government was unsure that it could rely on their support.

So the government changed its tactics. It decided to fight its war by arming militias from some of Darfur's Arab tribes, and letting them do the fighting for them. These militias became known as the 'janjaweed', and the Sudanese government's decision to make use of them is the main reason that the conflict in Darfur has escalated to horrific levels. It is argued that al-Bashir knew exactly what he was doing when he made this choice. Similar tactics had been used in the 80s against opponents of the government in the south, resulting in looting, violence against civilians, rape and torture.

The government has consistently denied that it has any connection with the Janjaweed militias in Darfur, arguing that the violence in the region is simply an outbreak of inter-tribal fighting. Whilst it is true that there are now many armed groups, many of whom may well be unconnected to the government, there is overwhelming evidence that the government is heavily involved with some of them.

Government officials are said to have recruited Arab militias with sackfuls of cash and the promise of development projects. Locals say that militia members are paid a salary of one hundred dollars per month by the government – far more than most Darfurians can hope to earn.

The army and military intelligence work closely with the Janjaweed during their operations. Human Rights Watch has documented many incidents where the Janjaweed militias and army forces have attacked villages side by side. The government says that these attacks are to flush out rebels, but there is often very little evidence to suggest that the targeted villages have any real connection with the rebel movement. It is enough that the villagers are from the same ethnic groupings.

The government has been adept at putting on a show of trying to end the fighting. It has set up a tribunal to deal with war criminals, but to date not a single high-ranking official has been investigated. It has carried out sham attempts to disarm the militias. In one of these it is alleged that the weapons collected were simply returned to the Janjaweed after the reporters had gone home. At other times, it has simply said that it is does not have the means to disarm the Janjaweed – a statement which may well be true but does not remove the responsibility for arming them in the first place.

At the same time, the Sudanese government also prevents independent observers from access to the area. Whilst it has allowed a small and inadequately-equipped African Union force into the area, it has consistently blocked the deployment of UN troops and it is notoriously difficult for NGOs to gain permission to work in Darfur – they can be quickly expelled if they criticise the government too openly. It remains to be seen whether it will go along with the most recent July resolution to send a 26,000 strong force. In 2004, when Kofi Annan visited Sudan to bear witness to the terrible conditions in its camps for Dafurian refugees displaced by the fighting he found that one camp had been evacuated just prior to his visit due to 'sanitary conditions' and another had been evacuated because of the threat of possible flooding in the oncoming rainy season.

It is unfathomable to me why the Sudanese government would actively pursue a policy that resulted in so much suffering. It is suggested that they underestimated the strength of the rebels, and that they thought the use of the Janjaweed would bring a quick solution to the problem. It also seems likely that they did not count on the international attention that the conflict has received. In addition, much of the government are kept in the dark as to what is really going on. It seems that the operation is managed by al-Bashir and a handful of his closest allies – whilst others are left out in the cold.

FURTHER READING

Burr, J. Millard and Robert O. Collin, *Darfur: The Long Road to Disaster*, Princeton NJ: Markus Wiener (2006).

de Waal, Alex, *Famine that Kills: Darfur, Sudan*, Oxford: Oxford University Press (Revised 2005).

Flint, Julie and Alex de Waal, *Darfur: A Short History of a Long War*, London: Zed Books (2006).

Johnson, Douglas H, *The Root Causes of Sudan's Civil Wars*, Indiana: Indiana University Press (2003).

Prunier, Gérard, *Darfur: The Ambiguous Genocide*, Ithaca, NY: Cornell University Press (2005).

http://www.hrw.org

http://www.crisisgroup.org/home/index.cfm

http://www.un.org/News/dh/sudan/com_inq_darfur.pdf

RUSSIA:
STORM IN A TEACUP

WHAT IS RUSSIA'S ENERGY WEAPON?

'Energy is like the nuclear weapon of the 21st century... Except it's better than nuclear weapons, because you can actually use it.'
Dr Bobo Lo., Head of the Russia and Eurasia programme, a Foreign Policy think tank

Contrary to what it sounds like, Russia's energy weapon is not a giant laser situated somewhere in Siberia. In fact, it is not a weapon at all – at least not in the conventional sense. When people talk about Russia's energy weapon, they are actually referring to Russia's control over a large slice of the world's energy supplies and the resulting pressure that Russia can apply to countries that depend on these supplies.

Russia, you see, has the largest gas resources in the world and is the No. 3 in the oil resources rankings. All this gas is effectively under the control of the government, as is about 50% of the oil. Gazprom, Russia's state-controlled gas company, controls more gas reserves than the seven largest Western energy companies put together. Its production levels are not a million miles away from those of Saudi Arabia.

Of course, 'energy weapon' sounds far more dramatic than 'influence by control of energy sources' – which is why journalists are fond of using it. It also has the immediate effect of putting Russia in the wrong. In the international arena, you are not meant to go around wielding a weapon.

It is not quite as cut-and-dried as that, though. Of the various situations in which it has been accused of using its 'weapon', the one that grabbed the most headlines was its argument with Ukraine at the end of 2005. Up until this time, Russia has supplied Ukraine with gas for 50 US dollars for 1000 cubic metres. They announced that they wanted to increase this price to 230 dollars – a large price-hike, I admit, but the average price in the EU at the time was 240 dollars.

The Ukrainian government refused to pay this amount to Gazprom. There was a stand-off – and then Russia made use of its 'energy weapon'. When Russia decides to take this course, it 'closes off the spigot'. Again, dramatic-sounding – but not so dramatic when you consider the action that these words describe.

If the 'energy weapon' was a conventional weapon, I imagine it would involve some sort of launching procedure by trained operatives, probably accompanied by countdowns and sirens. But what would 'closing off the spigot' involve? In my mind, I see a slightly-overweight man in overalls trundling towards a rusty lever with a wrench, the only sign of the perilous nature of his mission being a hard hat.

It is no joke being short of energy in the Ukranian winter and once the anonymous workman had done his job, it didn't take long for Ukraine to come to a deal with Gazprom. The two sides eventually came to a complicated compromise, involving shady Swiss-registered subsidiaries and Turkmen gas, under which Ukraine would end up paying 95 US dollars for its gas.

The Russian government came out of this disagreement very badly in the eyes of the world. It wasn't unreasonable to demand a higher price for their gas. There was no reason why Russia should continue to subsidise Ukraine's industry. It was more the aggressiveness of Russia's stance. In addition there was a feeling that this was not just an economic move. Many felt that the Russians were trying to influence the outcome of the upcoming Ukrainian elections by destabilising the pro-Western government of the time.

Ukraine is not the only state to find itself on the losing side of a disagreement with Russia over energy. In the past couple of years, Russia has cut off piped shipments of oil to Latvia in an effort to gain control over the port of Ventspils. Through its control over the pipeline network, the Russian government ordered that Kazakh oil be stopped from reaching a Lithuanian oil refinery in order to prevent non-Russian companies from buying it. It has also disrupted or threatened the energy supplies of both Belarus and Georgia. Nor is Russia's use of its energy resources a new development. In the early 90s, the government cut off supplies to the Baltic States in protest at their move towards independence.

Worrying as Russia's behaviour to its neighbours is, Westerners are more concerned about the possibility of Russia extending its aggressive use of energy resources to its relations with countries farther afield. The arguments with Ukraine and Belarus show that it is already capable of strongly influencing its neighbours. The concern now is that it will soon be in a position to do the same thing to Central European and Western European states.

In 2006, the EU already imported about half of its gas. Gazprom was responsible for 60% of these gas imports. Since gas is currently in vogue as a power resource – it is clean and cheap compared to coal and oil – the EU's gas imports are likely to rise. On top of that, Russia currently has control over all the gas pipelines to Europe, even if they are sometimes carrying gas from other countries, such as the Central Asian states of Kazakhstan and Turkmenistan. When Russia turned off Ukraine's spigot, it had knock-on effects on other European countries, disrupting their supplies.

It is highly unlikely that Russia will use its 'energy weapon' on the EU at this point in time. It relies too much on the cash it gets from the EU's custom to play that kind of game. It is even building a pipeline under the Baltic Sea direct to Germany, in order to stop any future arguments with its neighbours disrupting the EU's gas supplies again.

Still, people are worried about Russia's energy companies

having such a large piece of the EU energy market, especially since they are under state control. The EU has attempted to persuade Vladimir Putin to allow European companies fairer access to the Russian market without any success.

The EU is also attempting to diversify its sources. Many countries are reconsidering the option of nuclear power. There have been plans to build pipelines from the Central Asian States through Turkey, so that Russia no longer controls the whole pipeline network.

In response, Russia has been just as good at manoeuvring and has managed to reach an agreement with these same states under which they will continue to pipe the vast majority of their gas, if not all of it, through Russia for years to come. Putin is even trying to set up a gas-version of OPEC to give Russia and other gas-rich countries bargaining power in the international arena.

Whichever way you look at it though, it's not really an energy weapon – more of an energy bargaining chip. The danger is that its value is growing.

WHERE DID ROMAN ABRAMOVICH GET ALL HIS MONEY FROM?

'I love this game, I love this sport, I love this league. Why don't
I get my own team?'
Roman Abramovich

Roman Abramovich is the man who, seemingly out of nowhere, decided to stump up in the region of 400 million dollars to buy Chelsea football club and a team full of the world's best players. I read a report somewhere that said Abramovich shows visible emotion when he watches his team playing. Well maybe that is the truth but, if it is, I have never seen it.

When the camera scrolls across the crowd, it is always possible to pick Abramovich out. All around him children with scarves bounce up and down and men with fat bellies scream abuse at the referee, and there he sits, dead still, with an unfathomable half-smile turning up the corners of his mouth, as if he has been super-imposed on the football madness that surrounds him.

He gives nothing away. Apparently, he takes that smile with him wherever he goes. A journalist friend of mine once stumbled across it in the Kremlin. He fired questions at Abramovich for ten minutes, and all he got in response was the smile – except for one 'thank you', when he congratulated Abramovich on Chelsea's recent victory in the Premiership.

Pretty much all that is known about Abramovich nowadays is that he has a lot of money. According to one Russian finance magazine, he was worth 20.1 billion dollars at the start of 2007. He has all the usual billionaire trappings – houses all over the world, a fleet of luxury boats, a personal jet, a handful of helicopters and a go-kart track in his garden.

Abramovich grew up in the town of Ukhta, in the Komi Republic of north-western Russia. His mother died of an illness whilst he was an infant, and his father died in an accident a couple of years later. He was brought up by his uncle, who was an official in the oil industry. He served a stint in the army, and then studied at the Gubkin oil and gas institute in Moscow, after which he went about the business of making money in earnest.

His first venture was a toy cooperative. Next, he went on to make use of his uncle's contacts, trading oil and oil products. This was the 1990s – a time when Russia was trying to dismantle the old Soviet economy, and open it up to the free market. There was money to be made by people who worked out how to play the system. Abramovich was able to buy oil at low prices and sell it abroad at much higher prices on the international market.

It was a murky world. The rules of the game were so crude that it was possible to make huge amounts of money without necessarily breaking them. There have been no allegations of illegality against Abramovich – except for one minor enquiry involving a few truckloads of diesel that came to nothing. However, it was also a corrupt and violent world, and it is unlikely that anyone could have succeeded in it without using some strong-arm tactics.

As Abramovich became more successful, he came to the attention of some of Russia's main players. A handful of men, the so-called 'oligarchs', had made huge sums of money under the new economic system. With their money came massive political influence. Boris Berezovsky, a mathematician turned car-dealer, and one of the leading oligarchs, took Abramovich under his wing and decided to make him his partner in the purchase of the giant oil company, Sibneft, which the state was selling off as part of the infamous 'loans-for-shares' programme.

In this programme, private businessmen bid in an auction to

give loans to the government in return for which they received shares in various state industries. Whilst they were in possession of these shares, they were allowed to manage the company. If the government failed to pay back the loan, the individuals were entitled to sell their shares at another auction. Most commentators agree that everyone involved knew that the government had no intention of paying back the loans.

There are various theories put forward as to the reasoning behind 'loans-for-shares'. Some say that Russia's president, Boris Yeltsin, was buying the support of the oligarchs who controlled much of Russia's media for his presidential campaign for re-election in 1996. Some say that the government was just desperate for money – it was in the middle of an economic crisis and government workers had not been paid for months. Others maintain that the scheme was intended to take economic power out of the hands of the government.

On the face of it, the scheme doesn't sound like a bad idea. It certainly doesn't sound unfair. But it didn't turn out that way. The top oligarchs agreed amongst themselves who was going to get what. In most of the initial auctions, there was only one buyer. If unwanted competition turned up, ways were found to exclude it. For example, the company Norilsk Nickel was bought by ONEKSIM bank for 170.1 million dollars, barely above its starting price, despite the fact that a rival bank, Rossiiskii Kredit, put in an offer of 355 million dollars. It was ruled that it was unlikely that Rossiiskii would be able to honour its pledge.

The whole auctioning system was dubious. It was perfectly possible for a bank both to organise an auction, and also to bid in it. In the second round of auctions, after the government had not paid back its loans, there were several cases in which a bank sold its shares to itself in an auction at which it was the auctioneer. The starting prices for the industries were also obscenely low. In 1995 Norilsk Nickel had posted profits of 1.2 billion dollars.

In this shady business context, Abramovich and Berezovsky

turned up to the auction for Sibneft and received shares in it in exchange for a loan of just over 100 million dollars. Eighteen months later they bought these shares from themselves for pretty much the same price. A few years later, the company was worth a billion dollars.

After the purchase of Sibneft, Abramovich joined the elite group of the oligarchs, and he never looked back. He was on close terms with Boris Yeltsin, and he became the governor of the remote region of Chukotka.

At the end of 1999, Vladimir Putin took over from Yeltsin as President. Some of the oligarchs, including Berezovsky, had grown accustomed to meddling in politics. Putin resented this, and started legal proceedings against them. Berezovsky was forced to flee the country, and Abramovich bought many of his assets at rock-bottom prices, including his shares in Sibneft, a national TV station, Aeroflot (the Russian airways) and Rusal, the third biggest aluminium company in the world.

Abramovich managed to stay out of Putin's bad books, unlike other oligarchs. Even so, for one reason or another, between 2002 and 2005, he sold many of his largest assets, and took up residence in the UK, buying Chelsea in 2003. It is likely that his purchase of the club was not all down to his love of football. By doing so, he extracted a large chunk of his wealth from Russia. In addition, his new status as a well-known resident of the UK makes it much less likely that he will be subject to future criminal charges in Russia.

DOES THE RUSSIAN PARLIAMENT
HAVE ANY POWER?

'One man says to another on the train:
"Are you from the Kremlin? Are you from the KGB? Are you
from St. Petersburg? No? Then get off my foot?"'.
Russian joke

You would be forgiven for thinking that Vladimir Putin is the
only member of the Russian government. It is always his face that
stares out from the pages of the newspaper. It is an impressively
stern-looking face – a headmaster's face, I always think. And its
sternness is only enhanced by the knowledge that Putin spent
most of his early career in the KGB. He is also, by the way, a
very accomplished judo wrestler. He has a mean Haraigoshi – a
sweeping leg throw, which helped him become the Leningrad
city champion in 1974.

And yet there is a Russian parliament, which seems to be
in good working order. It has two houses. The Duma contains
representatives from several parties, elected by a mixture of
proportional representation and first-past-the-post electoral areas,
although in the next elections, only proportional representation
will be used. The Federation Council contains representatives
from Russia's many regions. All laws must be passed by a majority
in the Duma, and then approved by the Federation Council. The
two houses can reject a president veto, if they both vote to do so.
All very democratic.

But it doesn't really work in the way we would expect such a system to work because Putin pretty much has both houses in his pocket. As a result, they don't operate as checks on his power at all. In the whole time he has been in office, there has never been a time when either house has stood in his way on any issue of importance.

Under the presidency of Boris Yeltsin, the Duma, in particular, regularly challenged the president. In 1993, he had to send in the army to put down an attempted rebellion, after which a constitution was passed giving the president much greater powers. This action was the beginning of the end for an independent parliament, but, even after that, the Duma continued to oppose him. In 1999, it came close to impeaching him for various charges, including the destruction of the Soviet Union and his role in the conflict in Chechnya.

Since Vladimir Putin began in office, he has worked to ensure that parliament is compliant. He has gone about this task in a variety of ways, and he has been very successful. At the start of his presidency, the members of the Federation Council were the leaders of the governments in each of Russia's regions. Many of these were very powerful men, who ruled their regions more as monarchs than as elected officers. If a law was not to their liking, they felt strong enough to oppose it.

To get around this problem, Putin changed the rules. The leaders of the regions no longer came to the Federation Council. Instead, they were to nominate representatives. These representatives, without a power base of their own, were much easier for the president to manipulate. Putin also curbed the influence of these regional governors, by lumping together Russia's regions into seven massive districts. Each one of these was overseen by an official responsible only to the Russian president himself.

In 2004, Putin changed the rules for the elections of regional governors. From then on, they were to be nominated by him and approved by the regional parliament. In several cases, powerful and popular regional governors have lost their posts and been replaced by officials loyal to the President. Even before this change in the law, Putin had been able to influence regional elections in favour of his supporters. When Roman Abramovich, a Putin supporter, was campaigning for election as governor of the region of Chukotka, his rival was suddenly called in for investigation by the Moscow tax authorities.

So that was the Federation Council brought into line. But what about the Duma which was more influential than the Federation Council, and which had caused so much trouble to his predecessor? As it turned out, Putin didn't have to change any rules to bring the Duma into line.

There were elections for the Duma in 1999 and shortly afterwards there were elections for president in 2000. At the end of 1999, Putin became acting president. He was supported by Yeltsin and a powerful group of businessmen – the oligarchs – who were particularly worried that the Communists might regain power.

Yeltsin and the oligarchs understood that, if Putin was to become president, he must first control the Duma. As a result, they quickly put together a party, called Unity, which had no other purpose than to support Putin. In fact, this was true of nearly all the competing parties – they were simply vehicles for the various rivals in the presidential race. They had no real philosophy at all.

The oligarchs were the most powerful men in Russia. They had vast fortunes, and they controlled most of the media. They put all of their resources at the new party's disposal, and support for it quickly grew. Although Putin himself was not actually a member of any party, he made it clear that Unity had his support. A vote for Unity was a vote for Putin.

The tactics paid off, and Unity was successful, partly because Putin was credited with the recent victory of Russian troops in Chechnya. It did not gain a majority in the Duma, but by forming coalitions with other parties, it was able to pass anything of importance to Putin. In fact, several parties merged with Unity in 2001. They formed a new party, called United Russia, giving

Putin even more control over the Duma.

During the next elections to the Duma, at the end of 2003, Putin was able to take total control. By this time, the major TV stations and newspapers were back in state hands. In the previous years, Putin had challenged independent-minded oligarchs and won. They had all ended up in prison or escaped from the country, leaving the state to take over their media interests. As part of this same process, the state had also ended up with control over many of Russia's industries with all the money that they generated. In addition, Putin was still personally very popular with the Russian people. The other parties didn't stand a chance. United Russia ended up with a massive majority and Putin is now able to do as he pleases.

In a way, this whole process has been a democratic one. There were abuses of the system in both elections, but even if the elections had been totally fair, United Russia would still have been an easy winner, and Putin has won his presidential elections with ease. Throughout his presidency, he has remained incredibly popular, with his approval rating always above 70% – something that other leaders can only envy.

So, it is not as if what he is doing is against the will of the Russian people. It seems that Russians are happy to accept an authoritarian president if it means stability after a decade of infighting under Yeltsin, and if it brings wealth to the country. In a poll, only 1% of people felt that they had any control over their government, but this is not seen as a problem, just the way the Russian system has always worked.

However, Putin's control of the parliament is part of a general trend in which he has strengthened his control over all areas. When he came to power, the media was in the control of the oligarchs. Now it is state-owned. The same thing is true of many large industries. He has increased his powers over the judiciary, which had never been more than a mouthpiece for the state in the first place. There are no independent checks on the president's power.

As a result, he has been able to defeat potential rivals. For example, Mikhail Khodorkovsky, one of the oligarchs, was sent to prison in Siberia on charges of tax evasion. During the trial, there were allegations that defendants were injected with drugs, or questioned in the presence of hardened criminals, and that security forces had put in a threatening appearance at the school of Khodorkovsky's daughter.

I was surprised by the pessimism of the people I spoke to about Putin's methods of government, and the state of the government in general. They feel that, to all intents and purposes, Russia is a one-party state. In order to have any chance of success, it is necessary to be a supporter of Putin and United Russia.

Corruption is present at all levels. Officials support the system because it allows them to line their pockets. The legal system and security forces can be manipulated to bring about the downfall of any potential rival. The old oligarchs have been replaced by new oligarchs, who are just as unscrupulous in their dealings, but have pledged allegiance to Putin.

WHO KILLED ALEXANDER LITVINENKO?

'You may succeed in silencing one man but the howl of protest
from around the world will reverberate, Mr Putin, in your ears
for the rest of your life. May God forgive you for what you
have done, not only to me but to beloved Russia and its people.'
Extract from a signed statement by Alexander Litvinenko,
dictated 21st November 2006

It wasn't until I started researching the Litvinenko case that I
realised quite how bizarre his murder was. If it had been the
storyline of the new James Bond film, I would have criticised
it for being too far-fetched. That is saying something, bearing in
mind that, at the end of *Moonraker*, Bond is saved by a reformed
giant with metal teeth, who is prepared to eat through a metal
strut and consign himself and his pigtailed girlfriend to a lifetime
of romance in deep space.

Poisoning someone by slipping a substance into their cup of
tea is nothing new. Miss Marple was always investigating that sort
of thing. It is the choice of poison in the Litvinenko case that
makes it so strange. His killers decided to use Polonium-210, a
rare radioactive material. To get the amounts they needed for
their purpose, they must have had access to a nuclear reactor or a
commercial supplier of the stuff.

But why did they choose such an exotic method? Why did they
wander through the airports of Europe and the streets of London
with polonium in their pockets to put it in somebody's tea? There

are plenty of other, far simpler ways to go about an assassination – or so my contacts in the London underworld tell me.

Litvinenko used to work for the KGB, and then for the FSB, its successor organisation. Contrary to newspaper statements, he was never really a spy, but worked internally in Russia keeping tabs on its organised criminals. (Nobody ever seems to bother with the disorganised ones.) In 1998, along with several other colleagues, he accused his boss of ordering him to assassinate Boris Berezovsky, one of Russia's notorious oligarchs. After this, he was sacked and temporarily imprisoned before escaping to the UK via Turkey using a false passport in the name of 'Chris Reid'.

From 2000, Litvinenko lived in the UK, becoming a member of Berezovsky's anti-Putin circle. He made all sorts of claims against Putin and his former employers, the FSB. Some of them were credible. He was not the only person to suggest that the FSB had organised a series of mysterious bombings in Russian apartment buildings, which the government had blamed on Chechen separatists. According to this theory, the FSB carried out the bombings to give Putin an excuse to launch an offensive against the rebels in Chechnya.

Other accusations were more outlandish. Nobody took very seriously his claims that the FSB were linked to pretty much every terrorist organisation around the world. Importantly – and this is another reason why his murder is so unusual – he was not a major player in the dissident scene. There were – and still are – much higher-profile critics of Putin's regime.

The UK Crown Prosecution Service has charged Andrei Lugovoi, an ex-FSB officer, with Litvinenko's murder, and they have asked the Russian government to extradite him. The Russians have refused to do so, because the extradition of Russian nationals is forbidden under the Russian constitution. Their refusal should have come as no surprise to the British government. It is in line with international law and also with the assertive stance of Putin's government towards the world. Even so, it resulted in tit-for-tat expulsions of diplomats from the UK and Russia.

Lugovoi himself claims that he is being set up by the British secret services. Along with other ex-FSB officers, he met with Litvinenko in a fancy Mayfair hotel on the afternoon of November 1st. It was at this hotel that police later found a teacup with an off-the-charts radioactive reading. Radiation was also found on the flight Lugovoi took from Moscow to London to meet Litvinenko, and in the various hotels and restaurants he used during his stay in London. He returned to Moscow after November 1st – that flight too had radioactive traces – and then had to spend time in a clinic being treated for mild radioactive poisoning.

The Crown Prosecution Service clearly feels that it has enough evidence to bring Lugovoi to trial, but there are no clues as to what the motive was for the murder. There are plenty of theories though. Litvinenko and his friends pointed the finger at the Putin administration. Litvinenko signed a written statement on his deathbed to this effect. The Putin administration claims that it is a plot by Russian dissidents to discredit the president. Others suggest that it was an independent operation by the FSB – revenge for Litvinenko's treachery or a corruption cover-up. Or maybe Litvinenko was part of an international polonium-smuggling ring. Or maybe he was trying to help Chechen separatists build a 'dirty' bomb.

Conspiracy theorists are particularly fond of the Putin theory. They argue that Litvinenko is just the latest in a sequence of killings and poisonings. Four weeks prior to Litvinenko's death, the journalist Anna Politkovskaya was shot dead in her apartment building. She was an internationally-respected journalist and an outspoken critic of Putin, particularly with respect to the war in Chechnya. She was one of thirteen journalists who have died in suspicious circumstances during Putin's presidency up until the start of 2007. A counter-argument to this theory is Litvinenko's relatively low rank in the dissident scene. It seems to make little sense that the Russian government would go to such lengths to get rid of him.

The truth of the matter is that Russia is a dangerous place for journalists. There are plenty of people with secrets to hide. Litvinenko seems to have had connections to a number of stories that might have made him enemies. There were his initial accusations when he left the FSB and his continuing accusations during his time in the UK. On the very day of his poisoning he met an Italian journalist claiming to have information about the death of Politkovskaya. He had been part of an inquiry into alleged corrupt handling of investment funds by leading Russian officials. He had also claimed to have information about the Russian government's questionable break-up of the huge oil company, Yukos.

Litvinenko's death was front-line news because of its strange circumstances and because it happened outside Russia. We are unlikely to ever find out the motive for his murder, or an answer to why such a bizarre method was chosen, since the suspects in the case are never going to be put on trial. But what amazes me is that, if it had taken place in Moscow, it would have been just another assassination of somebody who had found out the wrong piece of information. Over the past years, to be an investigative journalist in Russia has been to sign your own death warrant. I had never realised what a shadowy and dangerous place the world of Russian business and politics is.

IS THERE STILL A WAR IN CHECHNYA?

'We'll follow terrorists everywhere. We will corner the bandits
in the toilet and beat the hell out of them.'
Vladimir Putin on Chechen extremists

I would have thought I'd know whether a major conflict had ended or not. It's a bit worrying if a war can just linger on without anyone much noticing its presence. Perhaps, we will discover that the Hundred Years War never really finished, and that the French have come up with a weapon more potent than the longbow.

For example, take the war in Chechnya. I remember that there definitely was a war a while ago, and that the international community disapproved of it. And then I remember that Vladimir Putin declared that it was finished. But then there was the horrific incident of the Beslan school hostage crisis, during which 186 children died in a gun-battle between Chechen separatists and Russian security forces, and the occasional report of further fighting in Chechnya itself. So maybe Putin had been premature in his announcement.

The Chechens have tried to set up an independent state many times in their history, but their recent efforts started in 1991. The Russians took a while to work out what to do about it, but eventually, in December 1994, Boris Yeltsin sent in the Russian army. The war was an inhumane affair in which, according to Human Rights Watch, around 40,000 civilians died, and Russian troops stand accused of torture and rape.

The Chechen resistance put up much more of a fight than

the Russians expected, making use of effective guerrilla warfare. Although the Russians took the capital city of Grozny and other important towns, they were unable to fully defeat the separatists, and finally they withdrew from the country in 1996. At this point, the two sides signed a peace treaty in which the Chechens agreed to remain part of Russia in exchange for more autonomy.

Peace didn't last long though. Provoked by bombings in Moscow and the meddling of Chechen separatists in an uprising in neighbouring Dagestan, Putin sent in the army again in 1999. This time it was more successful, and, by the end of 2000, the Russian army had retaken control of Grozny, signalling the end of open confrontation between the two sides. In 2003, a new Chechen constitution was passed, in which Chechnya was once again granted a significant degree of autonomy, whilst remaining part of Russia.

Putin managed to persuade the world community that the war in Chechnya was part of the global 'war on terror', claiming that his opponents were extremist Muslim terrorists with links to Al-Qaeda. By doing so, he managed to avoid the condemnation that met Yeltsin's invasion. Putin's representation is not really true. Whilst the separatists did receive funding from extremist Muslim groups, and whilst foreign Muslim militants were attracted to the conflict, the movement remained essentially a struggle by Chechens for a free Chechnya.

After 2000, Chechnya was governed by a series of pro-Russian presidents, who came to power after pretty dodgy elections, in which the separatist groups were not allowed to compete. But, as in the first war, the separatists were not fully defeated, and they continued to mount attacks, although the Russians and their Chechen allies did an effective job of assassinating most of their original leaders.

At this point in time, the stand-off continues. Ramzan Kadyrov is a tough leader, who took up the post of president at the beginning of 2007. By the age of sixteen, he was in charge of a unit of separatist fighters in the First Chechen War. His father, Akhmad, was a leading figure in the separatist movement at the time, but father and son changed sides during the Second Chechen War, and Akhmad Kadyrov became leader of Chechnya in 2000.

Kadyrov Senior was assassinated by rebels in 2004, and Kadyrov Junior swore to take vengeance. Although he has only recently become president, he has been effectively in charge of the country since his father's death, during which time he has met with a fair amount of success in maintaining its security. The rebels have been forced into hiding in the mountains, and they have lost more of their leadership. As a result, the separatist movement is currently fragmented, and capable only of launching occasional guerrilla attacks.

Still, Ramzan Kadyrov is no angel. He maintains his power with the support of his personal militia, the Kadyrovtsy, who have been accused by Human Rights Watch of torture, secret detention, and the 'disappearing' of enemies. He is essentially an 'absolute' ruler. There are no checks on his power. And despite the fact that Chechnya remains nominally part of Russia, Putin has given him unprecedented freedom in his exercise of authority.

Kadyrov has gained the respect of many Chechens through a combination of his ability to bring security to the country and a certain bling-factor. He owns a tiger and a lion, he has launched a Miss Chechnya contest and he has been visited by Mike Tyson. That, in my eyes, is an impressive amount of bling. It is unsurprising that the Chechnyan youth are won over by it.

And so, in a way, the war in Chechnya is over. Due to Kadyrov's ruthlessness, separatist attacks are on the decline. Grozny is being rebuilt with wads of Russian money. By handing over power to Chechen presidents, Putin has made the conflict an internal Chechen matter, rather than a Chechen-Russian conflict. This is one of the reasons why coverage of the war has died down – as well as the fact that Chechnya continues to be an incredibly dangerous place for journalists, and that Putin, with almost total control over the Russian media, does not want the continuing violence publicised.

However, it is also true that the separatists still exist. It is perfectly possible that Chechnya is experiencing a lull in the conflict, rather than a cessation. There is still plenty of ill-feeling towards the Russians around. Nor is it healthy that Kadyrov rules by force. It is also unclear whether the next Russian president will tolerate the current degree of independence that Chechnya enjoys.

In fact, neighbouring regions, such as Dagestan, Ingushetia and Ossetia, are already experiencing unrest, and there is a real danger that the Chechen conflict could spread throughout the wider region.

FURTHER READING

Baker, Peter and Glasser, Susan, *Kremlin Rising: Vladimir Putin's Russia and the End of Russia,* New York: Simon and Schuster (2005).

Hoffman, David, *The Oligarchs: Wealth and Power in the New Russia,* New York: Public Affairs (2002).

Jack, Andrew, *Inside Putin's Russia,* London: Granta (2005).

Wood, Tony, *Chechnya: The Case For Independence,* London: Verso (2007).

www.carnegie.ru/en

www.chathamhouse.org.uk

CHINA:
THERE'S ONLY ONE
PARTY IN TOWN

WHEN DID TAIWAN SEPARATE FROM CHINA?

'Whoever chooses to pursue Taiwan's independence,
he will not end up well.'
Chinese Premier Zhu Rongji, March 15th 2000

It turns out that this might not even be the right question to ask. It just goes to show how careful you have to be not to offend anyone in the field of international affairs. There are some who would argue that Taiwan has always been separate from China. There are some who would argue that the real question should be: 'When did China separate from Taiwan?' It all depends on how you interpret Taiwan's history.

Taiwan is a lush and fertile island – which is probably why the Portuguese christened it Ilha Formosa (meaning 'beautiful island'). Over the centuries, a variety of people have taken a fancy to it. Settlers from the Chinese mainland gradually populated it from the start of the 17th century, quickly outnumbering the Malayo-Polynesian natives. The Japanese have always had a hankering for it. The Portuguese, Dutch and Spanish all set up shop there at some point during the 17th century – although none of them lasted long.

From this time onwards, Taiwan came under Chinese rule – although some of the Malay natives in the mountains were never fully brought into line. In 1683, it became part of the Chinese province of Fukien, and over the next couple of centuries more and more mainland Chinese settled there. In 1886, it was granted the status of a separate province and in 1894, Taipei was made its legal capital.

But after China was defeated by Japan in the First Sino-Japanese War, the Japanese took over the island in 1895, despite the attempts of the Taiwanese population to declare their own independent Republic of Formosa. The Japanese crushed this attempt at independence, and went about the business of governing the island themselves. They built up the Taiwanese economy so that it became an important source of various products for Japan, but continued to treat the Taiwanese as second-class citizens.

Then came the Second World War, at the end of which the Japanese gave Taiwan back to China. This is where it all gets a bit complicated – because at this point there was a civil war in full swing between the Chinese Communists under Mao Zedong and the Chinese Nationalists (or the Kuomintang, KMT) under Chiang Kai-shek. It was the KMT that took control of Taiwan.

Initially, the Taiwanese population (most of whom were descendants of Chinese immigrants from the previous centuries) welcomed the change. However, it soon became clear that the KMT leaders were intent on governing the island for their own benefit. In 1947, the Taiwanese middle classes led an uprising, the aim of which was to force the KMT to grant the island greater autonomy. The 'mainlanders' put down the uprising brutally and declared a state of martial law, which lasted for the next fifty years.

By the end of the 1940s, it was clear that the KMT were going to lose the war with the Communists. Nationalist troops, officials and refugees fled to the island, and the KMT moved its capital to Taipei. So now there were two Chinas: the Communist-controlled People's Republic of China, comprising the Chinese mainland, and the KMT-controlled Republic of China, comprising Taiwan and a few of its neighbouring islands.

The international community, in particular the US, backed the KMT, anxious to prevent the further spread of Communism.

During the Korean War (which started in 1950), the USA stationed a fleet in the straits between Taiwan and mainland China. The USA continued to provide military support for the KMT regime over the following years. Until the 1970s, the international community refused to recognise the People's Republic, and it was the KMT that held a seat in the newly-formed United Nations – in fact it was one of the UN's founding members.

Throughout this period of time, the KMT government in Taiwan maintained that it was the rightful leadership of all of China, and that its eventual aim was to re-conquer and unite the mainland under its rule. However, as time went on, it became clear that there was little chance of such an event occurring. At the start of the 1970s, many countries severed diplomatic relations with Taiwan, and in 1971, it lost its seat in the UN to The People's Republic.

From the 1970s onwards, the KMT government began to relax the authoritarian control that it had held over the island since the uprising in 1947, although opposition to the KMT remained illegal. The Taiwanese began to take more important positions in the government, which up until then had been dominated by the Chinese who had come over from the mainland with the KMT at the end of the Civil War. The island also began to prosper economically.

In the 1990s, opposition parties were allowed for the first time, and in 2000, Chen Shui-bian was the first non-KMT leader to be elected president.

Currently, the status of Taiwan is unresolved. Although, to all intents and purposes, Taiwan operates as an independent state, the People's Republic continues to maintain that Taiwan is simply a province of China, and it appears as such in geography textbooks. Meanwhile, the KMT stick to the story that they are the rightful government of China.

You would have thought that the newer parties would come out and say that Taiwan is independent – but they do not dare to challenge the official story, partly out of fear of China's response, and partly because Taiwanese voters are in favour of keeping their links with the mainland.

According to academic opinion, China will eventually take control of Taiwan again, in the same way that it has taken control of Hong Kong. It has ousted the Taiwanese government from almost all of the organisations of which it was a member, and it has used its influence to prevent Taiwanese politicians from gaining access to the world's leaders. In particular, the USA no longer has particularly strong ties with Taiwan, and it is unlikely to want an argument with the rising power of China over this issue. So the academic money (which, let's face it, is the smart money) is that Taiwan will be Chinese again at some point in the next decade or two.

WHAT WAS THE CULTURAL REVOLUTION?

'Under heaven, all is chaos.'
Mao Zedong on the Cultural Revolution's excesses

The Cultural Revolution doesn't sound like such a bad thing. I was imagining enforced visits to the theatre, and a drive for proper pronunciation amongst the people. But it turns out that the Revolution involved neither of these. Instead, to my horror, I learnt that it consisted of giving all the teenagers in the country total power to do exactly what they liked.

I have spent several years teaching in schools. And I am aware that freedom is the last thing that you want to give teenagers. Fortunately, because they are not used to it, the reaction of Western teenagers to a taste of freedom is to drink cans of high-alcohol cider and to draw on one another's shirts. Chinese teenagers in the late 1960s were an altogether more potent force. They brought their country to its knees.

The Chinese Communist Party, led by Mao Zedong, took control of mainland China in 1949, founding the People's Republic of China. It has ruled the country until this day. In the 1960s, Mao began to worry about the communist movement and his position in it. On an ideological level, he was worried that it was creating its own class structure to replace the one it had destroyed. The Party's administrators were in the process of becoming a new middle class, enjoying the authority and privileges of their position. This all went against the spirit of equality that lay at the heart of Mao's interpretation of communism.

On a practical level, he was concerned that he was losing his grip on the reins of power. In recent years, he had launched a programme called the Great Leap Forward. In this programme, he had aimed to increase China's industrial output by organising China's peasants into communes, and encouraging them to carry out small-scale industrial activities. Unfortunately, the programme was badly organised. Peasants melted their own agricultural tools in order to produce greater quantities of steel, and their work in the fields was disrupted. It is estimated that around twenty million people died of starvation.

Unsurprisingly, the Great Leap Forward – and by connection, Mao Zedong – were criticised by some of the leaders in the Communist Party, who took it as a sign that able management rather than revolutionary zeal was the key to future development. But it was precisely this able management that Mao feared would create a new class structure. There was a danger that his own vision of communism would be sidelined, and his authority in the party undermined. In order to prevent this from happening, in 1966 he launched the Cultural Revolution.

The basic idea was to tear down the system and rebuild it from scratch with him at its head. He began to manoeuvre against his rivals, removing them from their posts and replacing them with his supporters. This included the promotion of his wife, Jiang Qing, to a position on the newly-formed Central Cultural Committee.

Next, Mao went about mobilising the urban youth. Schools and colleges were closed. Around ten million teenagers – high-school and university students – travelled to several massive rallies in Beijing. The state paid for their travel and accommodation. They were encouraged to challenge those in authority. Mao ordered them to root out those who were not staying true to Communism, and who were showing signs of 'taking the capitalist road'.

It wasn't very hard for Mao's teenagers – who he called the

Red Guards – to find signs of capitalism amongst those in authority. It probably only took a V-necked jumper or a side parting to convince them of someone's guilt. Their verbal attacks were brutal, and often became violent. It is estimated that around half a million died in the chaos. They forced suspected 'capitalists' to confess their crimes in front of crowds of their fellow-citizens, who hurled abuse and derision at them.

Mao had wanted a revolution, but, as revolutions tend to, it quickly spiralled out of his control. The Red Guards took over the Communist organisations in the cities, and promptly divided into factions and started to fight amongst each other in a competition to see who could be the most revolutionary. In this climate of unrest, nobody was safe. Political rivals began to denounce each other in the hope of furthering their own positions. During the Cultural Revolution, around 60% of Communist officials were removed from their posts, including some of the top-ranking moderates, such as Deng Xiaoping.

Finally, Mao had had enough. In 1968, the army was called in to restore order. The Red Guards were disbanded, and sent out into the countryside to keep them out of trouble. Meanwhile, the power struggle at the top of the party continued. Initially, the army men took the most important positions but Mao grew suspicious of them and kicked them out. Over the next few years, the radicals, including Mao's wife, Jiang Qing, and the moderates, led by Deng Xiaoping and others, battled it out, with Mao constantly changing his mind over whom he should support.

Eventually, after Mao's death in 1976, the moderates won the day. The leading radicals were arrested and brought to trial. Jiang Qing spend the rest of her life in prison, where she reportedly committed suicide in 1991. Deng Xiaoping became the most influential figure in the Communist Party, a position which he held for the next couple of decades. He was responsible for economic reform in China, introducing aspects of the free market which have led to massive economic growth. However, the standing of the Communist Party amongst the Chinese people was damaged by all the cynical infighting which led up to his eventual success.

WHAT LED UP TO THE MASSACRE IN TIANANMEN SQUARE?

'Some people crave nothing short of national chaos…
We must take a clear-cut stand and forceful measures to oppose
and stop the turmoil. Don't be afraid of students, because we
still have several million troops…'
Deng Xiaoping, Paramount Leader, April 25th 1989

It came as a surprise to me when I discovered that many academics credit Deng Xiaoping with successfully putting China on the road to modernisation. He was the main power in China from the mid-70s to the mid-90s and the only event that I associated with this period was the Tiananmen Square massacre in 1989. How could he be considered successful, if he was responsible for the deaths of anywhere between 900 and 3000 of his citizens?

Deng took hold of the reins after a decade of power struggles and chaos during the Cultural Revolution, in which Mao Zedong had encouraged teenagers to ridicule, beat and murder anyone they felt showed signs of not being revolutionary enough. There are few statistics available from this period, but it is estimated that around half a million people lost their lives and a hundred million were persecuted.

So, in 1978, when Deng took control, the country was in a mess. A Chinese peasant in 1978 was no better off than he had been in 1953. Half of the officials in the Chinese Communist Party had been disgraced and removed from their jobs – or purged, as the technical term seems to be. Since half the administration were cleaning latrines or undergoing 're-education', it was unsurprising that industry and the economy had gone to pot.

On top of all this, the Chinese people had lost much of their confidence in the Chinese Communist Party, the sole ruling power since Mao had led the Communists to victory in the Chinese Revolution in 1949. For years, the people had believed that it was infallible, and they had treated Mao as a god, bowing three times before his picture in the morning and relating the events of the day to him before they went to bed. However, over the previous decade, Mao chopped and changed his support from one follower to another. One day a politician was lauded as his successor, the next they were condemned as a capitalist traitor. As a result, the people no longer knew who to support.

Deng was all too aware of the situation in 1978. He realised that the Party's days were numbered unless he quickly got the people back on side. He decided that the best approach was to show the people that the Party could bring them wealth and improve their standard of living. In order to do this, he had to break with Mao's ideology, which had stressed equality and paid little attention to material goods. For Deng, 'it did not matter whether the cat was white or black, as long as it caught the mice,' – as a Chinese proverb would have it.

With the support of the other leading politicians, Deng made radical reforms. He brought most of the purged officials back to office. He improved the standing of the intellectuals, who had been targets in the Cultural Revolution (where they had been referred to as the 'stinking ninth category'), and gave them more freedom to generate ideas to help with the reforms. He gave provinces more control over their own affairs, and encouraged them to innovate in order to bring in wealth. He opened up China to foreign investment and concepts.

In the country, he broke up the communes which had been put in place during the Cultural Revolution. Peasants went back to farming on family farms. They were also given the freedom to set up light industry and grow a variety of crops. The result was bumper harvests. In the cities, Deng allowed more private businesses and began to break up or reform the inefficient state-owned enterprises. China experienced massive economic growth. In 1978, 250 million of its people lived in poverty. By 2005, that number had been reduced to 30 million.

Still, it was not all good news. The loosening of central control in China meant that some did better than others. The gap between the rich and the poor widened. Eastern provinces benefited from massive amounts of foreign investment and flourished. Inland provinces remained underdeveloped and full of poverty. The economic boom for the peasants faltered in the 80s. Millions of them left the land to look for jobs in the growing cities, where they lived in poor conditions and experienced discrimination. The break-up of the state-owned enterprises meant that millions of urban workers lost the safety net of a job for life, and had to deal with the insecurity of growing inflation and unemployment. There was a massive problem with corruption, as officials used their new independence to line their own pockets.

So, even though the country in general was much better off, plenty of people were still unhappy. The Party had set up a situation where its claim to power rested on its ability to provide its people with economic prosperity, and these groups felt that they were not getting their fair share. In the freer climate that the government had created to help economic reform, these people felt that they were able to voice their complaints – and they did.

In addition, China's new links with the world meant that foreign ideas trickled in through contact with foreign businessmen, trips abroad and various types of media. There was a growing feeling amongst intellectuals and students that economic reforms had not been matched by political reforms. Although the government had made some small changes to the rules – for example, villagers in some areas were able to vote for their local leaders – these were nothing like significant enough for supporters of democracy.

Initially, the leadership of the Party had been united on the need to bring about economic reform to lead China out of the mess it was in at the end of the Cultural Revolution. However, as the 80s wore on, there were growing splits between liberal politicians, who wanted to continue with reforms and were sympathetic to the students' views, and more conservative politicians, who were concerned that change was taking place too fast. It was not at all clear in which of these two camps Deng Xiaoping belonged.

It was against this background that the build-up to the demonstrations in Tiananmen Square took place. In early 1989, Beijing students sensed that the reforming politicians in the government were losing the battle. The government had announced its intention at the start of the year to tighten its control over the economy, and it showed no sign of considering meaningful political change. As a result, frustration grew on student campuses.

The trigger for the demonstrations was the death of the liberal politician Hu Yaobang, who had fallen from grace a couple of years earlier after a previous round of student protests. It was rumoured that he had suffered a heart attack, whilst he was arguing the need for further reforms with a conservative politician in the Politburo, the leading body of the Party.

Students started to gather in Tiananmen Square during the mourning process for Hu's death. As the day of his funeral approached, their numbers increased, until, on the night before his funeral on April 22nd, they numbered around a hundred thousand. The students demanded that the government recognise Hu's achievements. They also called for freedom of the press and an end to corruption.

The government was at a loss as to what to do. The split between reformers and conservatives remained, with the reformers arguing that the Party leadership should meet with the students and listen to their views and the conservatives arguing that this would be a sign of weakness and might lead to escalating protests. The government was not helped by the visit of Mikhail Gorbachev, which brought the world's press to Beijing and massive publicity to the students' cause. Gorbachev's visit was a disaster for the Party leadership. It was impossible to carry out the usual formal ceremonies because of the students' occupation of Tiananmen Square, where the Party headquarters were located.

The government's concern became more acute, when the protests began to spread beyond Beijing and beyond student groups. Journalists, intellectuals and even party officials started to join the movement, sensing that there was some sympathy for their cause in the Party leadership. Urban workers swelled the numbers, motivated by their concerns over unemployment, rising inflation, and corruption. Criticism of the Party became more direct, with demands for the resignation of Party leaders.

Faced with the escalation of the protests, the Party was forced into action. They were terrified that the demonstrations could turn into a revolution. They had seen how quickly China could slide into chaos if independent movements were allowed to escape government control, both in the Cultural Revolution and other periods of civil strife in Chinese history. For more recent parallels, the Party leadership only had to look at recent events in Communist Eastern European countries. On May 20th, it declared martial law. A couple of weeks later, to international outrage, the Chinese Army marched into Beijing and forcibly broke up the demonstrations.

For a while, it seemed as if the events of Tiananmen Square would bring an end to Deng's programme of economic reforms. However, Deng was convinced that the reforms must continue. China's economy continued to grow, until nowadays it is, by some measures, the second largest in the world. At the same time, Deng was adamant that political control must remain in the hands of the Communist Party, a conviction that his successors have held to.

Academics do not think that this state of affairs can continue. China's economic reforms have created entrepreneurs, intellectuals, unemployed and all sorts of other groups, none of which have access to adequate ways to make their views heard. It is quite possible that China will follow a course similar to other nearby Asian countries, where the growth of a middle class eventually allowed authoritarian governments to turn to democracy peacefully. Up until now, the leaders of the Communist Party have shown themselves to be resourceful and pragmatic, to such an extent that they are nowadays really only communist in name. How they will react to the changes to come remains to be seen.

WHAT IS FALUN GONG
AND WHY DOESN'T THE CHINESE
GOVERNMENT LIKE IT?

'Falun Gong is an anti-scientific, anti-human, anti-social,
anti-government and illegal organisation with all the characteristics
of an evil religion.'
Chinese Ministry of Foreign Affairs, August 1999

I have to admit that, when I first came across Falun Gong, I didn't
really take it seriously. I was working at an 'alternative' school
in New Mexico, and the class teacher decided that Falun Gong
exercises would make a good start to the school day. So, we all
stood in a circle, tensed our abdominal muscles and concentrated
on holding an imaginary rotating ball of energy in our hands. It
wasn't really my cup of tea.

It has to be said that there are some bizarre elements of its
leader Li Hongzhi's thought. For example, he thinks that aliens
have been living amongst us since 1900. He also claims to have
convincing proof of the falsity of Darwin's Theory of Evolution.
This proof turns out to be his 'discovery' that figures in ancient
cave paintings are wearing dapper suits and elegant hats. His
conclusion is that we are only the last in a series of civilisations
on the planet. Each previous civilisation has been wiped out by
some massive natural catastrophe which had left only a handful of
people to start the next one.

So, it came as a surprise to me when I read in the newspapers
in 1999 that the Chinese government had cracked down on the

Falun Gong movement, and imprisoned many of its leaders. I figured that there must be a bit more to it than I had realised.

Falun Gong is normally referred to as Falun Dafa by its practitioners. It follows in the footsteps of traditional Chinese regimes of meditation and exercise, which are designed to bring well-being to mind and body. Such regimes are called qi gong. In the 1980s, during which the Chinese government relaxed some of the rules and regulations that it had put in place as part of the Cultural Revolution in the late 60s and early 70s, qi gong once again became popular amongst the general population. The government encouraged it because it kept people healthy.

Qi gong was not considered a religion, although some of its variations did involve some spiritual aspects. The government continued to keep tight control over the religious activities of its citizens. Initially, the Communist movement had tried to get rid of religion altogether. When this proved to be impossible, the government recognised five faiths – Buddhism, Taoism, Catholicism, Islam and Protestantism.

Citizens were allowed to worship, as long as they worshipped the state-recognised versions of these five faiths. It was not permitted to have connections with religious bodies outside China – such as the Catholic Church in Rome. In 2000, Bishop Zeng Jingmu, who, at eighty-one, had only recently been released from prison after thirty years, was returned to his cell for refusing to recognise the state-controlled Catholic Church.

In the 1990s, a man called Li Hongzhi came up with a new version of qi gong, called Falun Gong. According to his version of his childhood, he studied with wise men from an early age, and was soon in possession of extraordinary powers. According to the government version, there was nothing unusual about him, except for a modest talent for the trumpet.

Li's new type of qi gong consisted of two strands: a study of his teachings and physical exercise in the form of five simple routines. Li promised practitioners that, through its practice, they would guide their spirits to a higher level and experience well-being in all aspects of their life. His teachings were explicitly moral. He wished his practitioners to lead more meaningful lives. However, Li continued to insist that Falun Gong was not a religion.

Whatever the truth about his childhood, Li was clearly an extranormal teacher. Falun Gong quickly had millions of adherents. At the turn of the century, the Chinese government estimated that there were two million practitioners in China, although Falun Gong organisations claim that it was more like seventy million. These practitioners came from all walks of life – and included plenty of government officials.

As Falun Gong grew in size, the government became jumpy about the influence it might have. It was suspicious of such a well-organised group. Despite claims to the contrary by Falun Gong leaders, Chinese leaders were concerned that it would use its influence to play a political role in the country. They were very worried about potential causes of social unrest. The 90s had already seen protests by peasants and laid-off workers at state-run industries.

As a result, the government began to turn against the Falun Gong movement. They suggested that it was a potentially harmful cult, citing as evidence some practitioners' refusal of medical treatment. (One of Falun Gong's alleged benefits was the cure of disease.) Li left China and set up shop in New York in 1998, since when his movements have become very secretive.

In April 1999, 10,000 followers assembled peacefully outside the Communist Party headquarters in Beijing to protest against the government's criticisms of their movement. It was not the first such demonstration – but it was on a much larger scale than previous efforts and in a highly sensitive location. The government broke up the demonstration forcibly and stepped up its campaign against Falun Gong, issuing a warrant for Li's arrest as well as arresting over a hundred of the movement's leaders.

The practice of Falun Gong is now illegal in China. Over the last few years, human rights groups estimate that tens of thousands of its followers have been detained, and that thousands have been sent to 're-education camps' for up to three years. Hundreds have been sent to prison.

There have been numerous reports from Falun Gong practitioners who claim they have been subject to torture, and there have been a number of suspicious deaths in custody, which the government, when it chooses to comment on them, puts down to 'accidents'.

The government campaign has been successful. For a year or two, Falun Gong practitioners continued to stage protests and to exercise in public. In 2001, a group of them tried to set themselves on fire, and in 2002 another group managed to hijack a TV station and broadcast anti-government messages. But now the movement has largely gone underground, and it has been left to practitioners in other countries to voice their complaints.

HOW DO YOU KNOW WHO IS IN CHARGE IN CHINA?

'A leader is best when people barely know he exists.'
Lao Tzu

It is a little confusing, from an outsider's perspective, if it is not clear what the top job in a particular organisation is. We all know that the president is the main man in the USA and that the prime minister is the top dog in the UK. Germany has its chancellor. Saudi Arabia has its king. Brunei has its sultan. San Marino has its captain-regent.

The same is not true for the People's Republic of China. It has a president, but the president has not always been the main power. It also has a premier, sometimes referred to as the prime minister, but he is not normally the No. 1 man. The General Secretary of the Chinese Communist Party is normally a post reserved for the overall leader, but Deng Xiaoping was the guiding force in Chinese politics from 1978 to 1992 without taking up this post, or the premiership, or the presidency. So how on earth do you know who to pay the most attention to?

The power in China lies firmly at the top of the Communist Party tree. At the national level, in Beijing, there are a series of bodies. There is the Party Congress, which is a huge body that meets every few years. The Central Committee is selected from the Party Congress. It is still large, and it only meets once or twice a year. Above the Central Committee is the Politburo, consisting of around twenty men, who meet on a regular basis. The Politburo appoints a Standing Committee, which has around five members, and meets nearly every week.

It is the men (and sprinkling of women) in the Politburo who are the main players in Chinese politics. The premier league of this group is the Standing Committee. These people control all the important positions in the Party, chairing the various committees that oversee different policy areas.

On the face of it, the government and the Chinese army are totally separate from the Party. The government has its own national institutions, such as the National People's Congress, which approves new laws, and the State Council, which is headed by the premier and contains the ministers of all the different ministries. The army too has its own structure.

In reality however, both the government and the army are controlled by the Party – although, since Mao, it has tended to take a more hands-off approach. The top government posts are all filled by members of the Politburo, who often have several jobs. The chairman of the Central Military Commission, which oversees the army, is also a leading Politburo member. In this way, the Politburo sits at the top of the Party, the government and the army.

So, at least we know where to look for the main man, but there are still twenty or so Politburo people to choose from, all jostling to manoeuvre themselves towards the top, as is the tendency of politicians the world over. It is possible to narrow the search down by looking at who is in the Standing Committee, since these are the real top dogs. There are also certain posts which are particularly important. These are the General Secretary of the Party, the Chairman of the Central Military Commission, the President and the Premier. Anyone who has a few of these to his name is definitely in the running for the top spot.

In the past, there was no doubt about who was No. 1. Mao Zedong dominated the political scene during his life, controlling every aspect of it. He decreed that he must personally approve every document issued by the Party's leadership. He was so domineering that he even influenced medical treatment given to his colleagues. When Zhou Enlai, one of the leading politicians of the time, was ill with cancer in the early 70s, it was Mao who decided the timing of his operations.

Since Mao, the Party leaders have made an effort to avoid such dominance, which is why Deng Xiaoping refused to take any of the top posts except for the chair of the Central Military Commission – although he was undoubtedly the main political force through the 80s.

In the last decade or so, it has become even harder to spot the queen bee. The Politburo is full of rival factions – reformers, conservatives, politicians from the wealthy coastline, politicians from the vast inland provinces – all of them jockeying for position, forming alliances and undermining opponents. In fact, these rivalries are the only real check on the power of the Politburo politicians, since there is no independent legal system.

It is generally accepted that Jiang Zemin succeeded Deng as the No.1 man. He held the posts of President, General Secretary and Chairman of the Central Military Commission during the 90s. At the present time, it seems that Hu Jintao is in the most powerful position, although the current premier, Wen Jiabao, is a definite rival. Hu has now taken exactly the same posts as Jiang did.

Still, Hu does not have the power to operate independently. He must work by seeking consensus with his colleagues and take into account the opinions of his rivals. Many of the politicians in the leading group are still loyal to Jiang. Experts say that it will be several years before it becomes clear who is really in charge of China.

FURTHER READING

Baum, Richard, *Burying Mao: Chinese Politics in the Age of Deng Xiaoping*, Princeton: Princeton University Press (1996)

Fairbank, John K. and Goldman, Merle, *China: A New History*, Harvard: The Belknap Press (2006)

Lieberthal, Kenneth, *Governing China: From Revolution to Reform*, New York: W.W. Norton and Co. (2004).

Saich, Tony, *The Chinese People's Movement: Perspectives on Spring 1989*, New York: M.E Sharpe (1990).

Smith, David, *The Dragon and the Elephant: China, India and the New World Order*, London: Profile (2007)

NUCLEAR PROLIFERATION: THE END OF THE WORLD AS WE KNOW IT?

WHICH COUNTRIES HAVE NUCLEAR WEAPONS?

'The gravest danger facing America and the world is outlaw regimes that seek and possess nuclear, chemical and biological weapons.'
President George W Bush, State of the Union Address, 2003

There is plenty of concern about the spread of nuclear weapons. Along with Iraq's alleged possession of chemical and biological weapons, it was the stated reason for the US decision to topple Saddam Hussein – even if it turned out that all he had was a few rusting artillery shells from the Gulf War. Since the Iraq invasion, attention has turned to the nuclear ambitions of Iran and North Korea.

In addition to that, there is always the fear that a terrorist group will get their hands on a bomb. Osama bin Laden has said that it is the religious duty of his followers to do just that and it is reported that crude designs of nuclear weapons and blueprints of US nuclear plants were found in Al-Qaeda hideouts.

Still, until recently the world has done a pretty good job of preventing the spread of nuclear weapons. In the twenty years after the Second World War, USSR, China, France and the UK joined the US in developing nuclear capability. Umpteen other countries considered following suit, but were persuaded not to do so.

When the Nuclear Non-Proliferation Treaty (NPT) was signed in 1968, these five countries were recognised as nuclear powers. They committed themselves to preventing the further spread of nuclear weapons and to reducing their own stocks with the eventual aim of eliminating them altogether. At the end of 2005, Russia still had around 16,000 weapons, whilst the USA had around 10,000. The other countries had a mere few hundred each. All the other signatories of the treaty – nearly two hundred countries at the present time – promised not to develop weapons.

Since 1968, there have been further successes. South Africa, which allegedly built six weapons on the sly under its apartheid regime, decided to destroy them all on the eve of its transition to a democratic government at the start of the 90s. It is currently the only country to have developed nuclear weapons and voluntarily destroyed them. South Africa went on to play a major role in setting up a nuclear-weapons-free zone throughout the whole of Africa. Libya and Brazil also elected to abandon nuclear programmes.

When the Soviet Union collapsed in 1991, Russia, Belarus, the Ukraine and Kazakhstan all inherited bundles of nuclear weapons, although control of them remained in the hands of the Russian president and military. Still, there were initial signs that the other countries might hold on to them anyway. Belarus made noises about doing so and the Ukraine had a parliamentary debate about it. Finally, after some intense diplomacy, all the weapons – more than 8,000 of them – were transported back to Russia.

But the NPT has not been totally successful. It is an accepted fact that Israel (which never signed the NPT) has had nuclear weapons since the late 60s – something that was confirmed when Mordechai Vanunu, a former Israeli nuclear technician, revealed details of the Israeli programme to the British press in 1986, for which he served eighteen years in prison. The Israeli government themselves refuse to confirm or deny the existence of their programme, preferring to stick to the ambiguous statement that Israel will not be the first country to introduce nuclear weapons to the Middle East.

In the last ten years, things have got considerably worse. India and Pakistan both announced themselves as nuclear powers with tests in 1998. Tensions between the two of them remain high and they have teetered on the edge of war on several occasions since then, occasionally engaging in nuclear brinkmanship. They have refused to sign up to the NPT, and it seems as if the world order has accepted their new status.

Abdul Qadeer Khan was the scientist at the head of the Pakistani nuclear programme. He also found time, possibly with the tacit approval of the Pakistani government, to run his own private black market in nuclear expertise and materials, exporting to Iran, Libya and possibly North Korea. He confessed to these activities in 2004, but has been pardoned by the president of Pakistan, General Pervez Musharraf.

In October 2006, North Korea joined the club of nuclear nations by detonating a nuclear device – although it was not a very successful test. North Korea was originally a member of the NPT, but withdrew from it in 2003. On top of that, there are concerns that Iran is also developing nuclear weapons, despite its continued membership of the NPT and its claims that it is only developing a civilian nuclear programme.

Although the NPT has been very successful up until recently, some experts worry that now we might be at the beginning of the end for nuclear non-proliferation. They are concerned that if, say Iran, develops a nuclear capability, then other Middle Eastern countries may decide to follow. The more countries that join the nuclear club, the more likely are the chances of both accidental and intentional nuclear war and the more vulnerable are stocks of weapons to terrorist movements.

During my research, one of my sources helpfully illustrated a scenario for an 'accidental war'. It was 'somebody pressing the wrong button'. The launch systems for nuclear weapons are generally a bit more complicated than that. Even so, I have a terrible image of a Homer Simpson character somewhere reaching out for a doughnut and accidentally pressing the red button. And yet for years, Russian and US weapons have been on alert status, capable of being launched in fifteen minutes. It doesn't bear thinking about – which is probably why most of us, most of the time, don't.

HOW CAN THE USA GET AWAY WITH HOLDING ON TO ITS NUCLEAR WEAPONS?

'You can't be a real country unless you have a beer and an airline – it helps if you have a football team, or some nuclear weapons, but at the very least you need a beer.'

Frank Zappa

It doesn't stand to reason. The United States is very keen to make sure that other countries aren't able to get their hands on nuclear weapons. It seemingly went to war with Iraq to prevent Saddam from doing so and continues to threaten Iran and North Korea for having nuclear weapon programmes. At the same time, it holds on to its own weapons.

You'd think that the Nuclear Non-proliferation Treaty (NPT) would have something to say about this. I mean, I imagine that the original aim of the NPT was not to have nuclear weapons dotted around the world. I would have thought that it makes no difference whether they are dotted around in Kansas or Kazakhstan. In my mind, it is the being-dotted-around that counts as proliferation.

Sadly, international agreements are not as simple as that. The NPT entered into force in the 1970s, and it currently includes all the nations of the world – except for Israel, India and Pakistan (who never signed) and North Korea (who withdrew in 2003). Some people argue that North Korea has not technically withdrawn from the treaty, but since North Korea thinks that it has, it doesn't seem to make much difference what other people say.

In its original text, the treaty distinguished between nuclear-weapon states and non-nuclear-weapon states. Nuclear-weapon states were defined as those countries that had exploded a nuclear device before January 1st 1967. It sounds to me like a dark version of the January sales. 'Hurry now and develop your nuclear status – one day remaining.' The lucky countries that met this criterion were the USA, the UK, the USSR, France and China.

Most of the NPT was directed at preventing nuclear weapons spreading outside this group of five. Non-nuclear-weapon states promised not to manufacture or acquire nuclear weapons, and accepted monitoring of any peaceful nuclear energy programme.

The nuclear-weapon states simply promised not to assist any of the non-nuclear-weapon states in getting their hands on weapons. They did not have to promise to give up their weapons themselves. They didn't even have to put their civil and military nuclear programmes under a monitoring system.

To this day, Russia and China have offered up few of their nuclear facilities for inspection and the USA is not perfect either. It strikes me as all very patronising: 'Don't worry about us, our governments are grown up enough to look after nuclear weapons. But your governments – well, that's a different matter.'

You might wonder why everyone else agreed to this state of affairs. There were plenty of other countries in the process of developing nuclear weapons at the time. Mostly, it was the result of the existing balance of power, with the two opposing superpowers prepared to put considerable pressure on their allies to prevent them from acquiring weapons. In return, the USA and the USSR undertook to protect their allies from a nuclear offensive. Pilots from non-nuclear NATO countries are still trained to carry out nuclear attacks. Non-nuclear-weapon-states were also promised assistance with the development of peaceful nuclear power programmes.

There is only one section in the NPT which puts any kind of pressure on the nuclear-weapon-states in relation to their own nuclear arsenals. It is the vaguely-worded Article Six, which calls for all signatories of the NPT to try 'to pursue negotiations in good faith on effective measures relating to cessation of the nuclear arms race at an early date and to nuclear disarmament.' It's all a bit up in the air. There is no mention of how to judge if countries are acting 'in good faith'. No specific steps to be taken. Just a hazy commitment in the general direction of disarming at some unspecified time in the future.

Unsurprisingly, the nuclear-weapon-states didn't take a huge amount of notice of Article Six, especially whilst the Cold War was in process. Since then, they have reduced their nuclear arsenals significantly, but the USA and Russia still have thousands of weapons ready for action. Certainly, the numbers of weapons have not been reduced to levels where we can all feel a little safer.

Even during the Cold War, some of the non-nuclear signatories of the NPT began to feel frustrated. They saw the NPT as a bargain. 'We promise not to develop nuclear weapons – you promise to give up nuclear weapons.' They felt that the nuclear-weapon-states were not keeping their side of this bargain.

After the Cold War came to an end, the frustration of these countries grew. In 1998, the New Agenda Coalition was formed by several important non-nuclear countries to pressure the nuclear-weapon-states into more efforts to disarm. There have been several motions at the UN General Assembly in favour of a convention to prohibit the use of nuclear weapons, which have been backed by around 150 countries. Such motions are always blocked by the nuclear-weapon-states.

There have been attempts in the last decade or so to strengthen the demands of Article Six. The original NPT only held for twenty-five years, and so, in 1995, there was a meeting of all the signatories to decide whether to continue it. It was not at all clear that this would be the case, not least because non-nuclear countries were unhappy with the lack of progress on disarmament by the nuclear states. Eventually, it was decided that the NPT would continue to apply, but only after it was agreed that there would be a greater effort towards reducing the number of nuclear weapons in the world.

In the 2000 meeting of the signatories – they meet every five years – clearer steps towards nuclear disarmament were spelled out. All countries agreed that their aim must be total elimination of nuclear arsenals and that there should be a body set up to monitor this process. In the meantime, the various countries pledged that they would work quickly towards bringing into force a Comprehensive Test Ban Treaty, under which all countries would promise not to carry out nuclear tests. They also pledged to work towards a Fissile Material Cut-off Treaty, under which all countries would promise not to produce more nuclear material for weapons.

This all sounds very promising. It looks as if Article Six has been replaced by something much clearer. There is a definite commitment to getting rid of nuclear weapons and definite steps put forward as to how to go about it. Sadly, it turns out to be one of these agreements that make you wonder whether diplomats and politicians ever feel that their daily lives lack any meaning. Presumably quite a few people spent quite a few days hammering out these details and some of them will probably have felt some kind of sense of achievement at the end.

But the USA has paid absolutely no attention to the 2000 agreements. In fact, it refuses to recognise their legitimacy. It says that the only standard by which it can be judged is the vague original text of Article Six in the NPT, and that, according to this standard, it is blameless. Worse than that, the USA has, in some areas, moved in the opposite direction from the 2000 agreements. It has failed to ratify the Comprehensive Test Ban Treaty and initially stood in the way of progress towards negotiating a Fissile Material Cut-off Treaty. The government's defence plans continue to attach considerable importance to their nuclear weapons. Without a change in USA behaviour, the other nuclear-weapon states are unlikely to modify their ways. Currently, the UK is the only country which continues to say that it will honour its commitments.

Maybe it doesn't matter. Maybe it is unrealistic to think that nuclear-weapon states are ever going to give up their weapons. I can imagine that any nuclear-weapon state is going to always want to hold on to one or two weapons – just in case. But there is a real question as to whether they need them. The nuclear-weapon states all have conventional military forces that are capable of overwhelming opponents in an armed confrontation.

Critics of the US government argue that its actions will eventually undermine the NPT and lead to its collapse. The US stance means that the partnership that brought about the NPT is at breaking point. Many non-nuclear weapon states may simply walk away from it. At the very least, they are unlikely to support US proposals to amend it in order to allow the tougher inspections which are needed to prevent countries like Iran from secretly pursuing a weapons programme.

Worse than that, the NPT relies on making the case to other countries that, at the end of the day, nuclear weapons are unnecessary. It is impossible to do this whilst the USA and the other nuclear-weapon states continue to argue that nuclear weapons are vital for their defence programmes. By doing so, the nuclear-weapon states only make it clear to other countries that nuclear weapons are highly desirable. Through their actions, they provide a convincing argument to other countries for the need to pursue a nuclear capability.

Or maybe it is not as bad as all that. Perhaps there is a future for the treaty. When the various countries meet again in 2010, both the USA and Russia will have new leaders, who may be prepared to negotiate further. Nuclear states will have to make clearer progress towards disarmament. Non-nuclear states will have to accept tighter controls on their civil nuclear programmes. It is clear, though, that changes will have to be made.

WHAT HAS LED UP TO THE NORTH KOREAN NUCLEAR CRISIS?

'We don't negotiate with evil; we defeat it.'
US Vice President Dick Cheney, December 2003

Whichever way you look at it, Kim Jong-il is an intriguing character. He is sensitive about his height (5 feet 3 inches) and wears special shoes and a bouffant hairstyle to make up for it. On diplomatic tours, he has been known to have fresh lobsters flown in daily, which he likes to eat with silver chopsticks in the company of beautiful women.

But neither lobsters, nor women, nor bouffant hairstyles hide the fact that he has kept the world guessing about his nuclear intentions for the last couple of decades. In October 2006, North Korea detonated a nuclear device for the first time, throwing the international political scene into confusion. Nobody knew how to handle a nuclear North Korea.

The nuclear test was another chapter in a long story of mutual suspicion and aggression. The Korean peninsular has been an uneasy place since its division into two separate countries after the Second World War and the subsequent Korean War. US troops remain in South Korea and there is a demilitarized zone between the two countries. South Korea and the USA are both still technically at war with North Korea. From its birth, North Korea has suffered from a siege mentality, building up its army and digging underground tunnels in order to protect the entire population from potential air strikes.

North Korea was persuaded to sign up to the Nuclear Non-Proliferation Treaty (NPT) in 1985, but it took years before it reached an agreement on the details of how its nuclear industry would be inspected. At one point, the International Atomic Energy Agency (IAEA), the body which monitors the NPT, sent the wrong agreement to be signed. The North Korean government let it sit on a desk collecting dust for several months, before sending it back. The IAEA then demanded that North Korea sign it anyway. The North Korean government considered this demand for several more months, before refusing to do so. It was a typical episode from North Korea's negotiating history.

Eventually, in 1992, an agreement was in place and IAEA inspectors flew in to check North Korea's nuclear programme. They found that there were flaws in what North Korea had said it had done. It looked like more plutonium had been extracted from its nuclear reactor than had been declared to the IAEA.

The IAEA accusations triggered a mighty row with the North Koreans, who gave the required thirty-day notice that they were withdrawing from the NPT. Twenty-nine days had passed, when the USA managed to finally hammer out an agreement that would keep the North Koreans on its side. It was called the Agreed Framework. The North Koreans promised to allow some IAEA inspections to continue and to freeze their current nuclear programme with the eventual aim of dismantling it. In return, they were given assistance in energy and security matters.

The Agreed Framework was signed in 1994 and within a couple of years it ran into trouble, as the USA and North Korea accused each other of failing to hold to their side of the bargain. Things took a decided turn for the worse when George W Bush came to power in 2000. His administration took a much more aggressive stance towards Kim Jong-il and his associates.

Bush allegedly referred to the height-sensitive North Korean leader as a 'pygmy' and included his regime in the 'axis of evil'. He accused the North Koreans of having a secret uranium enrichment programme, claiming that a top North Korean official had admitted as much. The North Korean government have consistently denied the truth of this claim, saying that the official's words were mistranslated. In his State of the Union address in 2002, Bush talked of possible pre-emptive military action against 'rogue states', holding on to the possibility of using nuclear weapons against them, in violation of USA promises made in the Agreed Framework.

In response, Kim Jong-il withdrew North Korea from the NPT at the start of 2003, restarted the country's frozen nuclear programme and broke the IAEA seals on stored nuclear materials – enough material to build several nuclear weapons. Since then, there have been continued attempts to find a way forward at six-party talks between North Korea, South Korea, China, Russia, Japan and the USA.

The six-party talks didn't really seem to be going anywhere fast until North Korea carried out its nuclear test. Since then, there has been more progress. In mid-2007, North Korea shut down its nuclear facilities again with the eventual aim of returning to the NPT and dismantling its nuclear weapons programme. In return, it will receive assistance for its energy sector and the USA has also guaranteed that it has no intention to attack it.

It remains to be seen whether the agreement will hold. Pessimists point to the endless past negotiations, which always ran into trouble. They say that it is unlikely that North Korea will give up its nuclear weapons, because nuclear weapons are North Korea's bargaining chip with the rest of the world. There is a strong argument to say that the USA has only paid attention to North Korea when it has played up the nuclear threat. It compromised in 1994, when the North Koreans threatened to abandon the NPT and it has compromised again recently, after the North Koreans carried out their first nuclear test.

On the other hand, optimists say that it is a considerable achievement that the parties have come this far. Many doubted that North Korea would actually shut down its nuclear facilities again but it has done so. They accept that the negotiations may take several years – they are already running behind schedule – but see no reason why they cannot reach a successful conclusion so long as the USA continues to focus attention on the situation.

WHAT IS IRAN UP TO?

'No civil nuclear programme can explain the Iranian nuclear programme – it is a clandestine military nuclear programme.'
Philippe Douste-Blazy, French Foreign Minister
BBC News, 16th February 2006

'Those who have used nuclear weapons in the past and by doing so, have created the most heinous of tragedies in the history of the human race, today are claiming to be the champions of disarmament. Iran's drive to have access to peaceful nuclear technology is what is rightfully ours.'
Iranian Foreign Minister Manouchehr Mottaki

A major problem for nuclear non-proliferation is that it is possible to work out that you can make nuclear power stations work – with everyone clapping you on the back and commending you for your dedication to science – and then use your newfound knowledge to help you make nuclear weapons – at which point everyone looks a bit awkward and remembers a prior engagement.

This is what plenty of people think that Iran might be up to. Iran itself insists that it is only trying to develop a self-sufficient nuclear power programme. In support of this claim, it points to the fact that it has signed the Nuclear Non-Proliferation Treaty (NPT), and that it has always allowed the required inspections to take place – although this is debatable. It has also frozen its nuclear programme voluntarily at times as a sign of good faith. On top of that, Ayatollah Ali Khamenei issued a religious decree against the development of nuclear weapons.

It turns out that it is very difficult to prove that Iran is not telling the truth. And, in fact, there are some players who seem inclined to give Iran the benefit of the doubt. China and Russia have been much less skeptical in the past about Iran's explanations than Western countries, although there is a feeling that they might not be totally unbiased – China is Iran's biggest oil customer and Russia has strong trade links with Iran.

Still, in the last year, the Director General of the International Atomic Energy Agency (IAEA), which polices the NPT, said that there is no conclusive evidence that Iran was trying to build nuclear weapons. Rather helpfully, he also said that it was not possible to rule this possibility out. In addition, he stated that, without extra inspections, it would not be possible to guarantee that Iran did not have a secret undeclared weapons programme. It is safe to say that he didn't overly clarify the situation.

Conclusive proof of a nuclear weapons programme is hard to come by. If it exists, it might be a non-nuclear aspect of the programme, hidden on one of Iran's military bases. The IAEA has no right to inspect these, unless Iran gives it permission to do so. It is not unreasonable for Iran to refuse to give this permission on the grounds of its own security, especially since the USA is making such aggressive noises. The whole thing is a bit of a pickle.

Even so, the international consensus is that Iran is up to something. It certainly hasn't played the game with a straight bat. Under IAEA rules, a country declares its nuclear facilities and materials and then the IAEA comes in and checks the declaration. As Iran points out, it has always allowed these inspections to take place.

In the summer of 2002, however, an Iranian opposition group drew notice to the fact that the government had left out a couple of facilities from the declaration, including a uranium enrichment plant. Not unlike an estate agent failing to mention that an apparently-attractive property has a bit of a dry rot and subsidence problem.

Since then, the Iranian government, whilst sticking to its legal commitment to the IAEA, has not helped to clear up the confusion created by the discovery of these new facilities. It has refused access to suspicious sites, prevented scientists and officials from being interviewed and failed to make adequate replies to the IAEA's questions.

In addition, there is a big question mark over Iran's claimed need to produce its own uranium for its nuclear power programme. Most other nuclear-powered countries import their uranium. Iran is only building one power station at the moment – several others are not even past the planning stage. It doesn't seem to make economic sense to put such money into producing uranium for such a small programme. Even more suspiciously, Iran's current uranium-enriching facility doesn't produce enough fuel for its one operating power station, leading to further doubts over its real purpose.

Against the background of all this suspicion, there are specific allegations made against Iran. Taken in isolation, no allegation amounts to much, but critics argue that taken as a whole, they are enough to raise serious concerns. For example, Iran was found to be manufacturing polonium, which can be used in the manufacture of simple nuclear weapons. Iran should have declared its polonium project to the IAEA, but it had not. It claimed that it wanted to produce polonium for space batteries, but since it does not have any space programme to speak of, critics are very dubious about this explanation. In 2004 a defector walked into a Middle Eastern embassy with a laptop full of documents for something called 'Project 111'. Amongst them were plans to redesign Iranian missiles and designs for sophisticated explosives and underground shafts – all of them potentially relevant to research on nuclear weapons. The Iranian government say that it is all a big hoax and refuse to discuss it. Western intelligence services think that the defector was genuine.

As a result of Iran's failure to answer its questions, the IAEA reported it to the UN Security Council at the start of 2006. In July, the Security Council – which includes China and Russia – passed resolution 1696, demanding that Iran stop its uranium enrichment programme. When Iran refused to do so, the Security Council passed two further resolutions, placing sanctions against Iranian trade in nuclear material and technology, and freezing the assets of countries and individuals associated with this trade. It threatened stricter sanctions in the future.

But although there is a feeling that Iran is hiding something, nobody is quite sure what it is, and, as long as Iran refuses to play along, it is unlikely that the picture is going to become any clearer. The established view is that Iran is aiming at a nuclear weapons capability, without quite going as far as actually building a nuclear weapon. This view contains a spectrum of possibilities. At one extreme, Iran could build and test all the components of a nuclear weapon and simply keep them stored separately. At the other extreme, it could use its peaceful nuclear programme to build up materials and expertise, which it could then use to build weapons in the future.

Because of all this confusion, there are various timelines given for when Iran could be in possession of a nuclear weapon. The most common of these is 2010, but all such calculations contain a number of variables and are based on incomplete information. The Israeli government has put out a figure of 2008. Other analysts say that it could be much longer. It is just not possible to say. Intelligence agencies have never done well in predicting when a particular country will achieve a nuclear capability.

What the majority of people agree on, however, is that Iranian nuclear weapons are not a pleasant prospect. The Iranian political order is not stable. It is unclear whether the present government have the experience to deal with the issues of nuclear status. There is a danger of revolution, in which case it is impossible to say who might get their hands on Iran's weapons. There is also the possibility that Iran's rivals might feel forced into producing their own weapons, undermining further the status of the NPT. None of these possibilities is good news.

FURTHER READING

Bodansky, David, *Nuclear Energy: Principles, Practices and Prospects*, New York: Springer Verlag (2004).

Ciricione, Joseph, Wolfstahl, Jon B. and Rajkumar, Miriam, *Deadly Arsenals: Tracking Weapons of Mass Destruction*, New York: Carnegie Endowment for International Peace (2003).

Forsberg, Randall, *A Nonproliferation Primer: Preventing the Spread of Nuclear, Chemical and Biological Weapons*, Massachusetts: M.I.T. press (1995).

Gardner, Gary T., *Nuclear Nonproliferation: A Primer.*, Boulder CO: Lynne Rienner Publishers (1994).

www.nti.org

www.ProliferationNews.org

www.globalsecurity.org

www.isis-online.org/publications/iran/index.html

GOODBYE

Well, that's it folks – for the time being anyway. My small window of time for finding out answers has closed. The school year has started, and I have returned to the classroom to try to persuade adolescents that multiplying fractions together is an important life-skill. It is a thankless task for which they will certainly not thank me.

Of course, the world has not stopped throwing up questions. The cauldron of current affairs is bubbling away. New situations are rising to the surface. There is growing tension between the West and Iran. Zimbabwe appears to be falling apart at the seams. The Pakistani president, General Pervez Musharraf, is struggling to keep control of his country. The Taliban are once again a force in Afghanistan. These are all situations about which I wish I knew more.

I enjoyed researching this book. My feeling of helplessness in the face of world events has significantly reduced. This is no vague assertion – I have proof. Recently, I watched an episode of 'Question Time'. The panel was discussing why the UK initially went to war in Iraq. The representatives from the Conservative Party and the Labour Party both insisted that the UK had intervened in order to prevent Saddam Hussein from continuing his repression of his own people.

A year or so ago, I would have accepted this, assuming that a politician was far more likely to have the facts at their fingertips than me. But, whilst I was writing the book, I did plenty of research on the arguments that the governments of the US and the UK presented to their citizens to justify the war, and I knew that, in this case, the politicians were misrepresenting the truth. Bush and Blair argued for war with Iraq on the basis that Saddam presented a definite threat through his pursuit of chemical, biological, and nuclear weapons of mass destruction. It was only after it was discovered that these weapons did not exist that they began to speak of the invasion as a humanitarian intervention.

I am a long, long, long way from being an expert on any area of current affairs, but it is comforting to know that at least now I have enough information to be able to tell if somebody is lying to me. Those two politicians were not being honest. I knew it. Likewise, I now know enough about global warming to take on self-assured people at barbecues who claim that the rise in temperature is all down to sunspots. They are wrong. Whilst sunspots may well have an effect on global temperature, it is not possible that they are the sole cause for the change in the world's climate over the past couple of decades. The scientific community is close to unanimous on this point.

Even more comforting than this is the knowledge that there are people out there who are perfectly happy to give up their time to help a current affairs novice like me to find some answers to their questions. Questions will continue to float into my head as I hurriedly read the newspapers before I head off to the work. Most of them, I am sure, will float out of my head before I can act on them. The difference is that now I know that I could find out the answers if I wanted to. And for this comforting thought, I am immensely grateful to all the experts who have helped me out over the past months.

ACKNOWLEDGMENTS

There are a bundle of people I would like to thank in connection with this book.

First of all, there are all the experts in the various different areas of my research, who somehow found time to put down whatever they were doing and patiently explain stuff to me. There are too many to mention them all by name, but the following deserve special credit for their endurance and understanding: Hugh Miles, Oliver Miles, Rime Allaf, Adel Darwish, Gareth Stansfield, Mark Pelling, Helen Clarkson, Kirsty Gogan, John Lyon, Matt Prescott, Adam Quinn, David Milne, Scott Lucas, Kristen Stoddart, Maria Ryan, Steve Mccorriston, Alex Jacobs, Allister Mcgregor, Tim Allen, Eric Neumayer, Katie Wright-Revolledo, Nathalie Butt, Tony Barnett, Dan Edge, Corinna Mullin-Lery, Laurs Camfield, Chris Phillips, Laleh Khalili, Lawrence Saez, Andrew Fischer, Oliver Bullough, John Russell, Fabrice Weissman, Angus Mckee, Julie Flint, Peter Mozynski, and James Acton.

Secondly, there is the team at Marion Boyars Publishers – Catheryn, Rebecca, Amy and Kit – who worked tirelessly to make sure that the writing process went as smoothly as possible. Thanks also to my agent, Laetitia, for her suggestions.

Thirdly, there is the group of friends who regularly emailed questions about current events to me. The majority of these questions were thoughtful and intelligent. Some of them were entirely inappropriate. This book is an elastoplast for your ignorance.

Fourth, there are the ladies from 'Loose Women'. I tuned in most days at lunchtime, and learnt more about the female sex than I realised was possible. I am not sure that this is necessarily a good thing.

Finally, there is Zac, who was my only real companion in the days spent at home tapping away at my computer. He never said very much, but I know he understands.

INDEX